The Fire of Love

Edwin Robertson

The Fire of Love
A Life of Igino Giordani
'Foco'
1894 – 1980

New City
London   Dublin

First published in Great Britain 1989
by New City London,
57 Twyford Avenue, London W3 9PZ
© New City London 1989

British Library Cataloguing in Publication Data

Robertson, E.H. (Edwin Hanton), 1912–
    The fire of love
    1. Catholic organisations. Focolare
        Movement. Giordani, Igino
    I. Title
    267'.182'0924

    ISBN 0-904287-28-9

Typeset in Great Britain by Chippendale Type
Otley, West Yorkshire

Printed and bound in Great Britain by
Courier International Ltd, Tiptree, Essex

Contents

To my wife
Ida
who also loved him

Preface by the Archbishop of Canterbury

I travel a great deal and wherever I go I have grown used to being greeted in each new place by flowers or messages from the local Focolare, always accompanied by the assurance of prayers. Though the experience is common, my appreciation grows no less. I have for many years admired the Focolare Movement and been grateful for its quiet ecumenism and witness to the simplicity of the Gospel.

Edwin Robertson is an outstanding European ecumenist; but he is not a man confined to documents and negotiations. He has a feel for the story of the personalities involved. Already he has written an attractive biography of Chiara Lubich and now provides us with a book which introduces us in a fascinating way to that other formative figure in the origins and growth of the Focolare Movement – Igino Giordani.

But Igino Giordani is not simply the servant of a movement. Of Igino, Chiara Lubich said in her eulogy after his death that he had been 'a Christian of the first order, a scholar, an apologist, an apostle'. In his early years he sought to serve his country as a Catholic patriot. In middle life, he became both an active politician and, at the Vatican Library, a pioneering cataloguer. Talented in many diverse ways and unusually articulate, none of this satisfied him. He chose instead to seek a simple way of following God.

Thus from 1948 until his death in 1980 Igino Giordani increasingly gave his time and energy to the Focolare. His vision and critical intelligence contributed effectively to the practical implementation of the original ideals of Chiara Lubich in the form of an ever expanding fellowship. The account of those years of his involvement, narrated in these pages with understandable admiration, is a shining example of saintliness in human life. I hope that in reading this story others are called to place their talents in God's hands and allow them to be used for the service of the Kingdom.

Robert Cantuar:

An Introductory Note by Tommaso Sorgi

*Director of
the Igino Girodani Study Centre,
Rocca di Papa,
Rome*

Before and after he died (in April 1980), numerous sketches of the life and character of Igino Giordani had already been published, both in Italy and elsewhere (Daniel-Rops in France in 1938, M.P. Williamson in New York in 1947). This biography by Edwin Robertson, however, is the first complete one to appear.

It is noteworthy for its attempt to locate the activity and thought of Giordani in the context both of the life of the twentieth century Church and of Italian politics in the period before the First World War and, later, in the period of the republican democracy. Still more admirable is the book's analysis of the personality of the man, which the author completes with intelligence and love. It is a gift he offers to all who knew Giordani in any of the various aspects of his life – in the family, as a politician, as a religious figure, as a man of culture. They can now discover him in his multiformity and completeness. It is likewise a gift for those who did not know him; they can now see him as a new witness to Christian humanism. It is a gift also to those causes to which Giordani consecrated his life. These causes were many: among them, in the first place, was the harmony between the divine and the social, the attainment of holiness by lay people, the unity of Christians, the spreading of the spirituality which he embraced when his own interior experience had matured.

The author of this biography knew Giordani; he spoke with him and was captivated by his many gifts and his inner life. He speaks of Giordani as a historian but also as a friend. Together with pages of subdued suffering because of his friend's passing, the author adds many others that communicate to the reader a tremendous respect for Giordani's many and always heart-felt commitments, his love for others and for the business of family and of social life, and even for the places of Giordani's childhood and work.

In particular, Edwin Robertson shows his admiration for Giordani's spiritual depths which prepared him for his meeting with Chiara Lubich in 1948, and for the new depths reached later when, having made the radical choice of a life of charity, he began a new interior journey as a member of the Focolare Movement. This is where a profound experience with God began, one by which Giordani became 'Foco': 'it was not a simple change of name,' Edwin Robertson writes, 'but a leap ahead in his spiritual life' (p. 154).

The biographer, then, manages to reconstruct the most important points of Giordani's new spiritual journey and of the important role he played in the Focolare Movement, both by quoting from Giordani's own writings and by a judicious use of the testimony of people who had worked with him. Giordani placed himself in an attitude of complete humility and of unity before Chiara Lubich, the foundress of the Movement, for in her he saw someone who had been given a special gift by God. He did this to such an extent that he too became a fundamental instrument for the very same special gift. He helped the newly-born Movement to present itself to the institutions of the Church. He opened the way for the entry of married people into the Focolare, a life they shared with celibates. He became the focal point for the Movement's activity on three fronts: the development of the family both on the human plane and as part of the community of the Church; the incarnation of the gospel spirituality in the life of the world, which sought to build a new humanity; and an ecumenism of a new kind, directed essentially at a mutual understanding between the Churches as they sought a common way ahead guided by love.

So far as the ecumenical field was concerned, however, in his early days Giordani had been rather polemical. Nevertheless, even at that time, there were signs of a particular attention to the initial strivings for unity, especially in England and America, among 'Protestants' – as, in those days, all who were not Roman Catholics tended to be called; this is put into relief by his biographer (pp. 107-108). In reality Giordani had a 'feeling of deep brotherhood towards non-Catholic Christians' (as he himself said in November 1939). This brought him to be one of the first Roman Catholics to realize the importance of 'seek; ig that which unites more than that which divides' in order to put oneself 'on the road where, if God wills, the baptized members of different Communions will be able to meet and walk together along this stretch of the *Via Crucis*' (as he wrote on 17th March 1944, while the Second World War was raging round about him).

Possibly it is this openness which has meant that the first person to write a real biography of Giordani is an eminent member of the Baptist Church. This is another sign of the new age that is dawning.

Edwin Robertson puts into relief also Giordani's role in the cultural field in Italy and his openness to other linguistic areas. Indeed, through his writings and conferences in the period between the two wars, he reached all the Catholic organizations and laity and came to be well known also in seminaries, monasteries and convents. He made, thus, a major contribution to the formation of the emerging leaders of the Church and of Italian society.

At the same time, he took his place among the representatives of European culture, and all over the world people benefited from the fruits of his reflections upon the Early Church Fathers and the social message of Christianity, and from his profound thoughts upon the Gospel. There were numerous translations of his works into a wide variety of languages, notably English (in the USA), and then Spanish (Madrid and Buenos Aires), Portuguese (Lisbon and Brazil), French, German, Czech, Serbian, and even Japanese, Chinese and Malayalam (Calcutta).

His intense activity as a journalist and writer was born from a passionate love of God and of humanity. As he looked back upon history, he saw how the denial of God is always translated into human loss and injury. Therefore he was determined to make culture an instrumnent for the diffusion of Christian values and he considered writing to be 'the highest form of the royal priesthood'. Seeing his fellow human beings disorientated by the most diverse ideologies and absorbed by materialism, he wished to help them by spreading various forms of enlightenment and with the vigour of his message. This message is the centre of the whole of his thought and consists in the rational demonstration of a fundamental fact: the Gospel is the seed of a revolution, *the* revolution, that has turned history upside down and that still today continues its work for the profoundest liberation of humanity.

The careful and loving reconstruction of Giordani's life by this English writer now makes Giordani, the outstanding man and Christian, available in a language known all over the contemporary world.

Very many people will thank Edwin Robertson for all his hard work.

Introduction

Igino Giordani was born in Tivoli on 24th September 1894 and died at Rocca di Papa on 18th April 1980. He was born into a family that knew real poverty. His father was a bricklayer, a devout Catholic and a hard worker; his mother was illiterate, 'who did not compose poems, but washed clothes'.* He died the esteemed and loved elder statesman of one of the most important spiritual movements of this century, a distinguished author of more than 90 books, a politician remembered for his incisive wit, his integrity and his large vision.

I first met him during a conference arranged by the Focolare Movement at Rocca di Papa, Easter 1978. I was there to present a copy of my new book 'Chiara', the biography of Chiara Lubich,† to the lady herself. She is the founder of the Focolare Movement and Igino Giordani was the first married man to join. She was generous in her praise of my little book which had described the origin of the Movement and her life with all its widespread influences within the Catholic Church, beyond it and into all the world. I had been present the year before in the Guildhall, London when she received the Templeton Award and it was then that I was asked to write her story. The presentation seemed a climax to my

* *'Memorie di un cristiano ingenuo'*, Città Nuova, Rome, 1981 p.18.
† 'Chiara', Christian Journals Ltd., Belfast, 1978.

work. Igino Giordani, I understood, would translate the book into Italian and this he subsequently did.

Although in my researches I had learnt a great deal about his part in the Movement, I had not met him. Now, on this platform at Rocca di Papa, he held my attention. This frail man with twinkling eyes spoke in such a way that you had to listen. That voice had held crowds and it still commanded attention, quietly, gently and with love. 'I wish I could be as good a *focolarino* [the name for a male member of the Focolare Movement] as described in this book', he said humbly. We spoke on the platform and off. In a number of meetings we grew close to each other. It soon became clear to me that I must write the story of this remarkable man.

I visited him twice more before he died and talked with him about his life. We retraced many of his adventures and he even went back with me to the Vatican Library where once he ruled supreme! In all my preparations for this book, I had his devoted help in answering all my questions. I grew to love him. 'My best friend', he called me and his eyes spoke more clearly than his words. When he died it was for me a bereavement.

Overture

The undying flame

When I visited him in 1978 and 1979, Igino Giordani was already in his 80s, a frail and gentle man, with eyes that showed his mind to be more than a memory. It was not the mind of an old man, lost in the past; he was still able to catch the excitement of new ideas. He read a great deal and brought the experiences of a long and active life to his reading with an intensity of concentration. He approached new books with the energy of a young man. He was no longer the feared controversialist that once he had been, nor did his pen devastate the arguments of those who disagreed with him, as once he had exploded the calumnies of Mussolini's brother against Alcide de Gasperi. But it would have been a mistake to regard his polemic, even in the gentle years of his age, as a dead fire. He had learnt a new gentleness since he became a much loved member of the Focolare Movement, but his keen analytical mind could still detect false reasoning.

He lived in honoured retirement, in a flat in Rocca di Papa, which belonged to the Focolare Movement. He was a member of the Movement, a *focolarino*. He went there shortly after his wife died. There are many parts of the Movement to which he has brought the energy of his mind in the years since he first met Chiara Lubich (17th Sept. 1948). A Movement whose example had been the three virgins of Nazareth – Jesus, Mary, Joseph – had extended to families, living the Ideal* in married life. He had the vision of the worldwide Church although he had much to learn about the ecumenical movement and was in many ways at first most fiercely Catholic and implacable against all heresies! Within the Movement, he had learnt to approach and understand his fellow Christians of other denominations. The Movement had enlarged his sympathy and he had brought to it his experience. As well as his leading part in the New Families Movement, he led the *Centro Uno*, the ecumenical work of the Focolare Movement. He contributed greatly to the rapidly growing Movement in its early years. He soon became known as a co-founder, with Chiara who had started it in Trent in the closing months of the War.

When I met him, others had learnt from him and taken over much of its direction. But he retained his involvement with *Centro Uno*, whose office in Rome he visited every week. He continued his work with the New Families Movement, which sprang from the increasing number of married members in the Movement.

Where he lived in Rocca di Papa, near Rome, was a small complex of houses, and an expanse of green grass, with a particular function in the Focolare Movement. It is a 'Mariapolis Centre'. The name comes from the gatherings in which the Movement's various small communities meet, usually in the summer, with others interested in what the Movement stands for: they call it a 'Mariapolis', or 'City of Mary'. At Rocca di Papa the Mariapolis Centre was built to hold conferences for the spiritual training of the members of the Movement.

Almost to the end of his life, Igino Giordani, known affectionately as 'Foco', would appear and often speak at

*The 'Ideal' is the Focolare Movement's name for its spirituality.

such conferences, even travelling further afield when his health permitted.

Both Tivoli where he was born and Rocca di Papa where he ended his earthly pilgrimage are within easy reach of Rome. I had intended to call the last chapter of this book 'Twilight in Rocca di Papa', but I was soon shown that his life there was more like a dawn than a sunset.

A life of great variety

In his long life which spanned so much of the 20th century, Igino adapted his mind and applied his will to a wide range of activities – and in all of them he emerged pre-eminent. He quickly took the lead at school and his first work with his father showed the making of a good bricklayer. With characteristic humour he looked back and described his life as a succession of failures. Before he had had time to become a good bricklayer, he said, they sent him to school; scarcely was he involved in the classical work of the seminary, when Pope Pius X closed down his local seminary and he was forced to attend a state school; a little more than a year as a soldier and, although he was gallantly wounded, his war was at an end; a short time at study and some successful examinations, the brief career of a schoolmaster and the political powers removed him; the beginnings of a successful career as a journalist and politician, then Mussolini progressed ruthlessly to power. And so it went on. Certainly, his life had been made up of a series of interruptions, but every time that he left one activity for another, he applied himself to the new activity as though it were his life's vocation. Any Italian living through the period that Igino lived through would find his life interrupted; but unlike many of his contemporaries, he saw closed doors as new opportunities to enter into new worlds.

19

After the First World War, in which he was thought to have ended his useful career before it had started, he progressed through different worlds – writer, librarian, parliamentary deputy (that is, a Member of the Italian Parliament), advocate for peace and opponent of NATO, until the crown of his life came in the Focolare Movement.

Throughout his various careers he had loved God and served his country. He was a devout Catholic with a vocation; he was in the best sense of that word a patriot. He was one of the earliest Catholics to see that to love God could be expressed in political service to Italy. He was among that small group that pioneered the way of the devout Catholic into the responsible politics of Italy. He was never a man to separate his love of God from his service to his country. Igino was born at a time when the Italian state was often regarded as the enemy of the Church and as a boy he saw how fierce was the opposition to the Jesuits in his home town of Tivoli.

The need of his youth was to serve Italy with integrity as a Catholic and an Italian patriot; the need of his middle years was to find peace for his country and serve it under conditions that would not involve him or his political party in compromise; the need of his later years was to become a saint in the sense that the New Testament uses that word.

The first need led him to Don Sturzo* and the *Partito Popolare Italiano*; the second, which was to find peace without compromise, led him back into politics, working with Alcide De Gasperi and the Christian Democrats as far as he could, reaching the climax of that part of his life with the moving appeal for peace and integrity in the Italian Parliament in 1948; the third, which had really been his life long search for saintliness, was fulfilled in the Focolare Movement.

* 'Don' is an Italian title for a priest.

20

The burning wick

Every attempt to quench the burning wick of this sensitive and brilliant man, who could turn his hand to almost anything and do it well, showed the undying flame of his spirit. In poverty and in political strife, in study and religious fervour, the flame shot up and told the world that he was alive. Very few men have made so great a contribution in so many fields. And this contribution has been made despite the circumstances which would have crushed any lesser man. Many a liberal soul was crushed by Fascism and Giordani had exposed himself more than most. There was a limited number of things that a liberal could do under a totalitarian government. He could escape and in exile prepare for the end of the regime; he could stay and suffer, perhaps to become a martyr; he could make terms for a while with a regime he hated in order to live after the regime had fallen, sharing the pain of the oppressive times with his people in order that he might have the right to a voice when all was over. Giordani chose a way which was peculiarly his own. He went abroad, not as an exile, but as an apprentice librarian. He learnt his library science in America and returned to fight Fascism from the Vatican Library. He even provided the opportunities for the Christian Democratic Party to hold its preliminary meetings before taking power after Mussolini was gone and the war was over.

Political action

It was after the First World War that Giordani began to play his part in Italian politics. He survived that war with a crippling wound which would have killed most men, but he continued his studies as an 'invalid'. He survived with a patched-up leg and a twisted right hand. He survived to teach, write and edit political journals in the turmoil of an Italy prepared for Mussolini. Under the influence of Don Sturzo, the priest who led the Catholics out of political isolation, he was soon in the leadership of the *Partito Popolare Italiano*, not a Church party, but one that supported the Church. Giordani insisted upon the separation, but mutual support, of Church and State. He was most successful as a political writer and the periodicals for which he wrote carried the clearest condemnation of Fascism and the most effective opposition. Such activity could not continue once the Fascists had power to crush it. Out of work and in poverty he sought a post in the Vatican Library. He equipped himself as a librarian and returned to reform the cataloguing system of the *Biblioteca Vaticana*, until it could be described as 'The most ancient library in the world with the most modern cataloguing system'. Almost every great library in Europe eventually adopted the system Giordani introduced.

While in the protection of the Vatican he used his library to shelter endangered politicians including De Gasperi, and he edited the monthly journal for priests called 'Fides'. This periodical was used to sustain their faith and its social implications throughout the Fascist period. After the Second World War he became a Deputy in the Italian Parliament until 1953. He early opposed the support of Italy for NATO, pleading for peace. His great speech in Parliament 'No! to War' * placed him against his own leader De Gasperi, but did not drive him into the arms of Communism. In fact, he refused to visit the Soviet Union because of the use they might make of his

* *No alla guerra*, speech in the Camera dei Deputati on 16th March 1949, Tip. della Camera dei Deuptati, Rome, 1949, pp. 23ff.

visit. His political influence was enormous, but he would not scheme for power.

An ecumenical Catholic

Six months in America had taught Giordani more than librarianship. He had met the other Churches. He had seen the Universal Church and broken out from the narrow vision of most Italian Catholics at that time. He was the first Italian layman to see the significance of the ecumenical movement – and that was in the twenties when few Protestants had yet discovered its importance! During the Fascist period he compiled a bibliography of the ecumenical movement which was unique and he wrote a powerful book on 'The Protestant Crisis and the Unity of the Church' (*Crisi protestante e unità della Chiesa'*), first published in 1930, although the first edition had several passages cut by the Fascists. He was a fiercely defensive Catholic whose articles in 'Fides' show that he could use all his polemics against Lutherans and Anglicans, but he learnt to broaden his own understanding of the Church. His intensive study of the Early Fathers, readily available in the Vatican Library, enabled him to approach the Orthodox Churches sympathetically and gradually he learnt the strength of other separated brethren as the journals from America, Germany and Britain poured into the Vatican Library.

Chiara Lubich

There was no doubt in Giordani's mind that the most important thing he did in the post-war world of Italy was not in the political field as such, but in his meeting with a

23

young lady from Trent on September 17th 1948. This young lady was Chiara Lubich, although at the time he was not quite sure how to spell her strange name. He wrote *Lubig* in his diary. The meeting was in a room of the Italian Parliament when Giordani was a deputy. Soon his attention was attracted. Her spirituality shone and yet she appeared so real.

He listened to her story of the Focolare Movement, this 'community at Trent'. It had started in the air-raid shelters, where a group of girls had read the New Testament and tried to live by the words of Jesus. There were many movements coming out of the terrible experience of the war and bombing and a few of them survived into the years of prosperity. They earned the name of 'air-raid shelter piety'. But this was clearly different and although Giordani learnt only a little of this community from the first meeting with Chiara, he recognized the difference. She was not like the usual pious people who came to seek his help. She was a devout Catholic in the main stream of Catholic piety – he recognized her piety as akin to that of the saints, particularly St. Catherine of Siena.

In later contacts with her he saw that she understood his longing for a recognition of the laity of the church. There were other points of interest and attraction: she had founded a Movement for unity because she recognized that the spiritual gift given to her was that of unity.

Chiara saw his deep spiritual longing and he saw the worldwide potential of the Movement she had started. There is no doubt that both saw the hand of God in bringing them together. Giordani said that it was the greatest day in his life. He helped Chiara to do what she had already seen as part of the nature of her call. He enabled her to open the Focolare to the world and to the Universal Church.

Within the Focolare Movement, he soon acquired the affectionate name of 'Foco'. It was and is used by the youngest in the Movement and to this day some of his family find it strange that so august a man should be spoken of in such familiar terms! But it was never a term of disrespect. It was a term of affection, and of respect for his deep spirituality.

Chiara gave birth to the Movement and is its continual inspiration, but Foco gave it a new breadth. How quickly Chiara saw this possibility when she agreed to his joining a Movement which at that time was largely of young women committed to a life of chastity in the world. Giordani saw at once that this step, the acceptance of a married man who was much involved in the political life of the world, gave to the Movement a new dimension.

This new dimension had been potentially there, but not able to find expression until he joined it. Chiara needed him. He wrote of that step from his own viewpoint:

> The presence of a married man (and of a politician at that) in the Focolare Movement meant that the label of 'outsider' no longer applied to someone who belonged to a part of society which was commonly excluded from virtue! . . . On entering the Focolare I finally fulfilled a vocation which I had felt for a long time. This was something which I was not able to accomplish in other Movements, even new ones, for they were more or less tied to a tradition which relegated the laity to a marginal position, almost like a spiritual proletariat.*

That comment is particularly striking when we recall that at the time of writing it Giordani was a leading Catholic layman, who had played a major part in bringing the Catholics out of their political isolation, a Patristic scholar of repute with many books to his credit,

* Lorit and Grimaldi, 'Focolare After 30 Years', New City Press, New York, 1976, p.57.

25

the editor of a journal which had sustained the clergy and kept them in touch with social and theological movements throughout the world during the isolation of most of them in Fascist Italy. In every respect, he was an outstanding and highly respected Catholic – and yet he could feel the deprivation of the laity and particularly those who were married – 'almost like a spiritual proletariat'.

When Igino became Foco all that changed!

The new dawn

After the death of his wife, Igino Giordani came with his little suitcase and knocked at the door of what was to be his new home in Rocca di Papa. Giordani knew it well and had come to where he already belonged. He was gladly received and it was there in his flat that I shall always remember him. There we talked for hours about the experiences of a rich life. There he operated at the centre of the whole Movement, travelling, but more and more working from his own room and the office of *Centro Uno* in Rome. He directed that centre until his death, edited the journal, 'Città Nuova' which has its equivalent in many countries and languages, always under some such title as 'New City'. He watched over such Movements that radiated out from the centre as 'New Families', 'New Humanity', etc. He was at the centre of it all and much in demand to speak at conferences, always received with joy and affection. Even in his 80s he could still inspire large meetings.

As I saw him in his flat at Rocca di Papa, he was surrounded by his books. Among these are the official biographies of 'Pope Pius XII', the most controversial Pope of modern times, and Alcide De Gasperi, the architect of the post-Fascist Italian state. Shelves carried long rows of bound copies of 'Fides' and 'La Via' which bear witness to his journalistic skill. For among those copies you will find many articles bearing his name and even more written by him under a pseudonym! His walls were hung with pictures that showed his love of beauty and his deep affection for Chiara and the Focolare Movement. On his table and in intriguing drawers and cupboards were treasures and tributes which shyly he brought out when pressed.

As I sat and talked with him there, I marvelled that one man could have encompassed so many lives and done so much in each of them. In his own mind, however, the richest and dearest part of all these 'lives' and in some way, the climax to which they were all leading, was the final years in which he had lived within the obedience of the Focolare Movement. There he attained his saintliness and lived by the words of Jesus. To his mind, the Movement had given him everything he ever sought. He was satisfied that he had attained his goal when he lived simply as a *focolarino*, like any other member, playing his part as he was able. His contribution was immense and that last period of his life was a dawn which prepared him for the entry into a fuller consciousness with God through death. The grandchild that laid the flowers upon his grave seemed like the little gift he had left behind for those of us who found not loss, but a new sense of unity when he died. His grandchild is one of a new generation of the Focolare.

The Focolare Movement did not bring wealth and fame such as his political career or his writings might have done. Indeed some thought a great man had wasted himself on a religious movement. But he recognized that without wealth and fame, the Focolare Movement had brought him love and life and honours far greater than would have been his had he become Prime Minister of Italy or Nobel Prize Winner for Literature or Peace.

A few years ago, his home town of Tivoli honoured him as 'most distinguished citizen'. He showed me the award, but I detected that the honour of being a *focolarino*, loved by the youngest in the Movement, touched him more deeply. In the light of this new dawn, honours like everything else looked different.

Part One

The Making of Igino Giordani

1

Tivoli

Tivoli is a small town rising up from the river Aniene, to the east of Rome, among the Sabine hills. It boasts an antiquity older than Rome and claims to be the site of the mythical 'rape of the Sabine Women', from which Rome sprang. Its Latin name is Tibar and a little boy from Tivoli would be a *tiburtino*. At first sight, it seems impossible to reconstruct the Tivoli of eighty years ago. The medieval town which lasted unchanged for centuries, growing steadily and suffering from a landslide which took place early in the 19th century, was recognizable at the beginning of this century when Igino Giordani was a child. Today, Tivoli is a dormitory for those who work in Rome, or a place for tourists to stop as they visit Hadrian's Villa or wander among the fountains of the Villa D'Este a few miles away. The vineyards and the olive groves have been swallowed up by large buildings, blocks of flats where the homes of more than 300,000 people swarm over the surrounding hills. Yet, the older part of the town where Igino lived is little changed.

A pilgrimage to Tivoli

His simple home was in *Via Maggiore* near by the church of San Antonio. The name of the street has been changed. The home has been pulled down and one day something may be built there, and perhaps there will be a plaque to say that IGINO GIORDANI lived there. San Antonio stands still, but appears to be derelict and unused, forsaken by the local inhabitants. The cobbled streets run by, as slippery as they were in the days when his mother carried him down to the river to wash clothes, and as cold and windy on a winter day. One of Igino's earliest memories is that of biting into something warm and soft that he thought was bread. He recalls that rocking journey on his mother's back as one in which a philosophical thought was born. All innocent of Heraclitus, he felt the swaying body of his mother, saw the streets running by, the flowing water of the river, the precipitous bank caused by the famous landslide, the fear of falling, and concluded that all things were in a flux! This journey of a hundred yards down to the river was an adventure for him. And it was not long before he was making even more adventurous journeys into the surrounding countryside. As a small boy, he often seemed to have been lost. Later his exploring spirit led him into alien territory where a *tiburtino* might be in danger. On our pilgrimage we found the scene of one such adventure. It was in San Gregorio da Sassola.

We were in search of something Igino had helped to build when he was a boy. The bridge which led into San Gregorio was the scene of an incident Giordani remembered well. It was when he was 13. When we saw some big boys roaming round and looking for something to do, we recalled that incident when Igino had gone off on his own. As he crossed the bridge some boys, just like those we saw, remembering a feud with Tivoli, called out 'Here comes a *tiburtino*. Let's throw him in the river!' Igino was terrified and had visions of his body floating down the river, then picked up later by a sorrowing family. He stood his ground and like all bullies they turned away.* But what was he doing so far from Tivoli?

The *'piccola vasca'*

When he was about 13 Igino often helped his father and proved valuable in sharing the work. I asked him if anything remained of his work as a builder. He thought not. Perhaps the *'piccola vasca'*, he said. That had been built somewhere near San Gregorio da Sassola. It was on a white *'edificio'*, he said, not far from Santa Maria Nuova. It was probably then that he met the bullies on the bridge. But we wanted to discover whether the *'piccola vasca'* still existed. Exactly what it was we were not sure – a little basin, perhaps a fountain. The white 'edifice' would help us to find it. In Tivoli we found a bridge called Ponte Gregorio, crossed it and came at last, much further than we had expected, to San Gregorio da Sassola. It looked like a stage-set, a completely walled town, set high and grey. Inside the town were no roads that a car could take. There were stepped roads cutting across the town, old and cobbled. It was typical of many Italian hill towns which have remained unchanged by the centuries. It must have looked just like that in Igino's day. There was something almost sinister about it and we shared something of Igino's fear on that bridge. More to the point of our search, we could find no white 'edifice' and no Santa Maria Nuova. We remembered that Giordani had said: 'in the commune of San Gregorio da Sassola'. We continued along the road and then asked a workman. He told us that Santa Maria Nuova was further along and with that familiar Italian courtesy

* *'Memorie'*, op. cit., p.35f..

33

escorted us until we could see a church across the fields. 'There it is – across the meadow', he said. We marvelled at its isolation. There was nothing else in sight. No houses, no people. A church for what? We discovered that it was a monastery. But there was no white 'edifice' and no *piccola vasca*. We were discouraged. Giordani had thought it would probably be destroyed and apparently he was right. It was a monk at Santa Maria Nuova who gave us fresh hope. He had been there for 43 years and he remembered an old spring which had watered the fields since the Middle Ages and where the villagers still went for water in the heat of the summer. Perhaps we would find our *piccola vasca* there. We did.

The white 'edifice' was a pretty pair of Gothic arches in white stone. They formed two doorways into a cave. There three troughs or basins had been constructed at various heights, so that the spring water flowed into the top 'basin' and then overflowed into the others in turn. The lowest was outside and easily available. All three troughs were full and overflowing when we were there in the winter, but I would imagine that in the heat of summer, the troughs inside were cool and kept from evaporating. An ingenious scheme and well constructed. We convinced ourselves that it was Igino's *piccola vasca*. To complete our joy we found violets blooming on either side and picked them for Foco. His work had not been destroyed and it was useful still. That seemed highly appropriate for a work of Igino Giordani!

The confraternity

In Tivoli we also visited the church of S. Andrea where the young Igino had been taken by his father to attend the meetings of the confraternity. In those early years of the

34

century there was no 'Catholic Action' in Tivoli and the only opportunities for laypeople to deepen and express their faith in an organized Movement was through the confraternities. There were three in Tivoli – one for the upper classes, two for the working class! Such terms were permissible in 1900! Foco had told me of these meetings which he had attended as quite a small boy with his father. Together they would say the offices in Latin and sing: 'How we sang', he said, 'we yelled!' Those meetings meant much to him. They were times of real involvement with the Church and with his father.*

The church of S. Andrea is set among narrow streets and has changed as little as its immediate neighbourhood. It is in the old part of the town, only a few minutes walk from where the Giordanis once lived. The narrow streets are full of poor and crowded houses, twisted like an old oak tree, with little colour. Then as now the brightest spot in that section of town is S. Andrea. Inside it was lit up and kept in good condition. An energetic little boy was running about the church, blowing out the candles for the priest. Eighty years ago, little Igino might well have done just the same – the church was his familiar palace, brighter than the dark home from which he came. But where did the confraternity meet? We searched and found an irregular shaped room behind the vestry, untidy and cluttered with things the church had once used and did not wish to throw away. It was like any other church hall of a small church, used at times for table tennis and the youth club, but this was the one where Igino had sung with his father and carefully pronounced his Latin words. Another find in that room was a faded photograph of the interior of the church in 1904. It had been taken when the church was decorated that year for

* ibid. p.27.

S. Lucia's Day. That was how the church appeared to Igino at 10 years old. Apart from the special decorations for the day and relaying of the floor, little has changed. There someone heard Igino pronouncing his Latin rather well and thought he should have further schooling.

Schooling in Tivoli

An Italian film, called in English 'The Tree of the Wooden Clogs', portrayed village life in Lombardy at the end of the last century. There is a little boy in that film who has been noticed as rather brighter than average. It is suggested that he would profit from some schooling. The father discusses the matter with the priest and after much heart-searching decides that the boy should go to school, even though none of his family had ever done that. It was a revolutionary decision. It must have been equally difficult for Igino's father to decide that a strong young man of 13 should leave him and go to school. But he did so decide. The elementary education was understood and Igino had learnt the rudiments of knowledge for a working boy – all he would need if he were to follow in his father's footsteps as a bricklayer. The rest his father would teach him. Further schooling would be a departure from normal practice. It was Antonio Facchini, the local pharmacist who thought Igino was worth supporting. He paid for his schooling on the recommendation of someone who had heard him pronouncing his Latin well and no doubt from his own observation. It was a sacrifice for the father who would have to give up this extra help. But he too saw something more than the average in young Igino.

At 13, Igino went to the *Seminario*. The teaching was strict, in the hands of priests and with an emphasis on

Patristic writings and classical languages. Igino was overwhelmed at first, but soon his natural, rebellious spirit arose. Long afterwards he could remember his protest against one sentence from the priests: *'la donna è il demonio'* (woman is the devil)* How could that be? Was his mother a devil? Was Mary a devil? That was not the last of his questioning. He learnt quickly and never questioned the basic framework of his Catholic faith, but he questioned the opinions thrown at him. The mind that later would be so penetrating was already being formed in the teenager. It was a search for truth within a stable framework of acceptance. All his life, Igino was to remain a loyal Catholic, but ever ready to question what appeared to him to be phoney – wherever he found it!

The first dislocation

As the result of a plan to tidy up the educational systems of the Church, Pope Pius X closed many local seminaries, keeping only the efficient regional schools. This could have proved disastrous for Igino, because one of the local seminaries to close was that at Tivoli. A very limited number of places were made available in Anagni, but the majority would have to leave school or go to a state school. In the later part of the 19th century, education in Italy had been developed both by Church and State separately. There was no doubt in anyone's mind that the Church schools were of much higher quality and as Dr. Hearder, no friend of the Church, admits 'schools run by the religious orders remained the best'. Only one of the 30 boys at Tivoli was fortunate enough to go to Anagni. The rest including Igino went to

* ibid. p. 39f..

what we should have called at that time 'the local grammar school'. It is difficult to appreciate the break that this meant for young Igino. The idea of the priest-hood had already attracted him and passing to a state school was something of a betrayal. We need to recall that the Catholic Church had not really accepted the Italian State, and there were devout Catholics who still regarded it as the enemy of the Church. The Church was kept out of politics, and Igino had already been involved in a struggle in his own Tivoli between the Jesuits and the liberals who drove them out. He must have felt as though he were passing over to the enemy. He described it as 'almost an act of disloyalty'.* His early sense of vocation never left him, but he did not fully understand it until it was realized in the Focolare Movement much later.

Crises of adolescence

At the new school, and probably aggravated by the secular atmosphere and the influence of totally new teachers and quite different values, Igino passed through the usual crises of adolescence. These held him back from the religious life. He pointed out that it was not only the usual objections to dry and sentimental piety, to celibacy and obedience to authority, but certain worrying intel-lectual doubts and cultural difficulties. As the world of culture opened up to him he found the attitude of the Church narrow. The young bricklayer had come a long way when he found it difficult to accept the elementary explanations and the medieval credulity. The influence of secular and even anti-clerical teachers upon him began to tell. He mentions Lino Vaccari who taught him science,

* ibid. p. 43.

never pausing to consider the Church's objection to the theory of evolution, and Salvatore Multineddu was a Communist, who broadened his mind and changed his way of thinking. There were other teachers, many anti-clerical and the principal who was a Freemason. It was no wonder that at this stage he began to give up his practice of religion. Meanwhile, a very patient and uncomplaining benefactor watched the young man whom he had financed, apparently losing his faith in simple religion.

There is nothing unusual in this story of a young man fascinated by the new world of ideas and culture, finding his simple faith and credulity inadequate for the experience of a larger world.

A Catholic in secular Italy

At the state school, the *convitto nazionale*, which still stands four-square in Tivoli, like a fortress rather than a school, he was provided with food and lodging in return for some work as a tutor. There he obtained his qualifying certificate with sufficient honours to seek for a job. He sat for a competitive civil service examination and was soon on his way to a post in Rome. He was appointed clerk, third class, with a salary fixed, according to a decree of 10th September 1914, at 1500 lire. This was a princely salary and far more than his father would ever earn. It meant travelling to Rome on the steam tram every day.

At the age of 10, he had been taken to Rome for his confirmation, but that had been a frightening experience from which he had fled twice because of rumours of what might happen to him. Now he would travel into Rome each day, rather more than an hour's journey, with others who had important jobs in the capital. He must have felt that his career was beginning. But enough has been said already about this young man to make clear that he is not going to be satisfied with the routine work of a civil servant. He was bursting with ideas. As a Catholic he was also entering hostile territory. There was as yet no Catholic party in Parliament and Rome was a secular city, more so because of its defiance of the Vatican City in its midst. Church and State lived in uneasy tolerance of each other.

The school had taught him to think. He was an avid reader and he had political ideas. He was a Catholic in more than a nominal sense: he was also a patriot, but not uncritical. The conflict between these two made life difficult.

These were the stirring days of Gabriele D'Annunzio, fiery speeches and the prospect of war. Igino had little sympathy with the entry into a war which seemed to mean nothing to Italy and which could only interrupt his career before it had even started.

The 19th century had pitted the Vatican against the Italian State and Igino was caught in the crossfire. The Vatican regarded the Italian State as aggressive in its improper acquiring of Papal lands and its incursions into education; on the other hand, the Italian State regarded the Vatican as a hostile state within its borders which might at any time reassert its old political power. Italy was still predominately Catholic and its people devout, but in the political field there were old sores. Thus priests and those associated with them were not expected to take part in politics. The effect was that devout lay Catholics found other jobs and did not concern themselves with political affairs. They had no natural Catholic party to which to belong. Leadership of the state thus passed into the hands of those hostile to the Church and was often anti-clerical. The fact that today Italy has the largest

Communist party in Western Europe is partly due to that period of Catholic isolation from politics. This began to change when Don Sturzo, a priest of Sicily led a Catholic political party out of that isolation. That party would eventually play an important part in Igino's development.

Meanwhile he led a tranquil life of a commuter going daily to work for several months, until the First World War brought Italy and Igino into its destructive process.

The making of Igino

Before we rush this young man into the enthusiasm and destruction of war, let us look at him awhile and see what has made him what he now is. First of all, the devout family life of poor people. We know little of Igino's mother, but all we know shows how careful she was of her boy. In any Italian home the mother plays a caring role, sometimes spoiling the boy. Igino's mother seems not to have done that and the dominant influence seems to have been that of his father. It was with him that Igino worked, attended church and the confraternity meetings. It was he who gave up the help a strong lad could have provided in order to allow him an education. There is no doubt about the sacrifice of letting a boy go to classes instead of work. A poor home, and Igino's was at times a very poor home, needs all the help it can get.

The Church also played a great role in making Igino. He grew up informed and devout. The *seminario* gave him opportunities and taught him how to study. But one Church influence was considerable, that of the Jesuits and particularly Father Mancini. Igino's father had a great respect for the Jesuits who came to Tivoli, and he supported them when many attempted to get them out of town. Igino was deeply impressed and took their part

41

against the fellow citizens of Tivoli who were anti-clerical. Looking back Giordani wrote of these trouble makers that they were 'frequently the illiterate, fortified by cheap red wine and harangued by communist agitators in the drinking shops and bars'.* The confraternities had brought the Jesuits to Tivoli and Igino shared his father's admiration for them. In some notes written many years later, Giordani recalls something of the magical effect of these earnest and devout men upon the young boy:

> I saw the two fathers once in a festival when the church of S. Andrea was studded with lights and crowded with people, catching a glimpse of the procession through a door in a pyramid of lights. The lights trembled in the apse, shining through the mist of gold and silver shadows. Only one who was totally without feeling could refrain from a little shudder of excitement or keep his hat on his head. Even the Socialists doffed their caps a little. And I rejoiced to have Jesus on the altar and Father Mancini in the pulpit!†

He remembered that scene so vividly and recalled the enthralling preaching of Father Mancini, 'drinking in every word without missing a single one'. It is perhaps worth quoting at length from some notes Igino Giordani made about that period when he was so susceptible to the influence of these magnificent Jesuits so that the effect upon him on their expulsion from Tivoli can be understood. This is obviously one of the major influences upon his young life and played its part in the making of Igino:

> My father had prepared me for Father Mancini and his colleague: two religious men, somehow connected with the church of S. Andrea. From the way in which my father talked of them, and my mother echoed, they appeared to be two super-human beings, equipped with

* ibid. p. 28.
† ibid..

knowledge and wisdom, sacred instruments and victorious defenders of the faith.*

His father had given him and the neighbours the impression that these two wonderful creatures were quite invincible. It was therefore a very great shock when the news came that they were to be evicted from Tivoli.

For a month, as he bent over the pot of fire, full of glowing embers around which, in the middle of the kitchen, we kids gathered together with our grandparents and neighbours, my father, depressed yet still with a shadow of hope, foretold the feared departure of the Jesuits. His voice, with the tone reserved for solemn occasions, vibrated with a sorrow as of some terrible family misfortune. I, by reflection, was in consternation. I too was persuaded that it was not possible to go on without Father Mancini, and I longed for I know not what punishment to be visited upon those responsible.†

A little later, Igino and his father went to a secret meeting with the Jesuits.

They were in a kind of attic, whose windows looked out upon the moss-green rooves of S. Andrea, except one widow that, from the inside, looked down upon the flickering red of a lamp in the midst of a haze of gold and violet. It was the apse of the church, which seen from above blazed like a strange basin filled with stale sun. And all that I saw made my sadness more painful.

I remember that a thin, black priest caressed my bushy hair, and I kissed his waxen hand. My father was embarrassed. The next day they left.‡

A little later, Ignio was to be taken to Rome to the magnificent church of the Jesuits and to feel again the fascination of Father Mancini and witness the active opposition which he aroused among the enemies of the Church.

* ibid. p.28f..
† ibid. p.29.
‡ ibid..

The commuter to Rome

The simple piety of the poor, the gorgeous splendour of the Church, the intellectual stimulus of school and the Jesuits, all this and more went into the sophisticated young man who took the steam tram to Rome seeking his fortune. It was ten years after the departure of the Jesuits but something had burnt into his mind which would not be erased. The influence of Father Mancini never left him.

2

The First World War

When the 20 year old Igino Giordani travelled to Rome for his first post at 1500 lire a year (£250 in the currency of the time – a reasonably good starting salary), Europe was already entering the most destructive war in history, known for many years as the Great War. Italy was in the midst of intrigues, but not yet involved. She wanted to be rid of the tyranny of Austria over some of her Italian lands. Different parties were seeking to obtain this, the one by glorious war to win the 'unredeemed' territories of the north from a reluctant Austria; the other by promising to stay out of the war to receive those territories as the price of neutrality. By 1915, Italy was in the war on the side of the Allies, with promises of all she wanted after the war was won. Igino watched the move to war without enthusiasm. He was patriotic, but not a militarist. As a devout Catholic he would be thought by some to be suspect, because such Catholics were thought to have loyalties to the Vatican, which might conflict with the loyalty to the glories of Italy.

In 1915, the patriotic front was strong in Italy; the stimulus of Italian literature, much of which was anti-Austrian, the letters and poems of Gabriele D'Annunzio, the desire for glory and a late entry into the scramble for colonies, the vexed question of Italian-speaking territories like Trentino still under Austria, all this added up to patriotic fervour and a pressure to 'drive out the Austrians!'

Conscription

Young Igino was less concerned than most of his age with the promised glories of a restored Roman Empire. He had worked hard to get where he was and had no desire to throw it all away in the futility of war. He was neither a war supporter, nor a war protester. His main concern was to make a career for himself in the Ministry to which he had been assigned and to work conscientiously without exhaustion. He was not caught up in the enthusiasm of much of Italy's youth, for he could not view with any great excitement the prospect of all his studies and his parents' sacrifices leading to cannon fodder.

He did not feel enough ill will towards any Austrian to want to kill him. He saw the absurdity, the stupidity and above all, the sin of war. The sin seemed the greater because of the pretext upon which Italy was to enter the war and the futility of the way in which issues of national pride were to be decided.

Igino Giordani in 1915 was a young man wishing to live according to the high principles of his Catholic faith, to be obedient to the teaching of Jesus and follow the example of the saints. As a layman, he would live as faithfully as he could in the world. All his life he sought the role of the faithful layman as an honourable part of the Catholic Church. For him, 'layman' was not a negative description of someone who was not a priest; it was a positive description of one of the people of God. The Gospel to which he remained faithful all his life had often enough said that one must do good and not evil, save life rather than destroy it, forgive rather than take revenge.

He was a young man trained to use his reason. The measure of absurdity of the proposed entry into the war was patent and only hidden by patriotic fervour. He could see that the fruits of victory would not be awarded to those who had the most right on their side, but to those who had the most cannons. The issues would be decided not according to justice or natural rights, but by violence. He was unmoved by the call to extend Italy's borders into Germany and Austria and equally unmoved by Salandra's call to *'sacro egoismo'*. All his training had taught him that *egoismo* was never sacred. He was not a volunteer!

Igino Giordani, like so many other young men, was called to arms, after the events of 'the glorious month of May', 1915 when Italy entered the war. He was conscripted on 11th June 1915.

He went convinced of the stupidity of war, angry at those who were sending the youth of Italy off to a meaningless death. Gabriele D'Annunzio did not inspire him, but bored him.

Italy's road to war

Igino was not alone in his opposition to entry into the war. Those who wanted Italy to get involved, the *Interventionists*, were a minority. Even Salandra, head of the government in 1915, admitted that war was 'conceived and wanted by an active and courageous, but in all honesty, an infinitesimal minority that the government could very easily have controlled'.* On a number of occasions, the Holy See had shown its preference for Italian neutrality. The majority of Catholics, the Socialist

* Max Gallo, 'Mussolini's Italy', MacMillan, New York, 1973; Abelard-Schuman, London, 1977, p.40.

Party and the workers who formed the bulk of its support all favoured neutrality.

Those who wanted war were mostly minority pressure groups: some students of middle-class origin, nationalists, some sectors of the business community and the press (though 'La Stampa', 'La Tribuna', 'L'Avanti', 'Il Mattino', and the Catholic Press all spoke out against war). Together with them were several revolutionary intellectuals, and even a few syndicalists and some Socialists who were influenced by the movement to regain the lands of Italian speakers under Austrian control.

The *Neutralists* had an impressive leader in Giolitti. But in 1913, Salandra's conservative liberal group had broken away from Giolitti's progressive liberals. The two men interpreted the possible effects of war differently. Salandra wanted entry into the war to avoid revolution and he thus had the support of the right wing Interventionists. At that time, revolutions were thought to come only from the left! Giolitti was convinced that one of the effects of war would be the birth of revolution. In this he was proved right.

The decision was influenced not by debate in the Chamber, but by demonstrations in the streets. The demonstrations were mostly for war, the Interventionists gradually gained possesion of the streets and they produced the most dramatic figures. There were also demonstrations to keep Italy out of the war, mostly by Socialists and there were soon clashes between Socialists and Interventionists. One of the first serious clashes occured in Milan on 25th February 1915, when some people were injured. Then in Reggio Emilia, two men were killed. Public demonstrations were prohibited on 29th March, Parliament was adjourned and Salandra had a free hand.

Meanwhile two separate negotiations were going on without reference to each other. Sonnino, the Foreign Minister was negotiating with the Austrians for compensation as the price of not entering the war. Giolitti imprudently spoke of this as having gained something really important (*parecchio* – which means 'a great deal', 'really something'). The Austrians had agreed to almost all the Italian demands. The fruits of non-intervention seemed so much more certain than the promises of the Allies. On 4th April 1915, 'L'Avanti' published the terms of what Giolitti had called *parecchio*. The foolishness of going to war after that was beyond belief. But Sonnino had been talking to the Allies also since 4th March. And on 26th April he signed the secret Treaty of London with England, France and Russia. This treaty granted Italy's demands for a frontier at the Brenner, Trieste, Istria and the greater part of Dalmatia and the Adriatic islands. It also referred to 'legitimate colonial compensations'. This was very substantial, although it was mere promises to be granted after the war had been won. And with this treaty, Italy agreed to enter the war within a month of signing. Only three men knew of this secret treaty – Sonnino, Salandra and the King – and these three had committed Italy to war before 26th May. Giolitti, leader of the majority party in Parliament knew nothing of it, neither did the Chief of Staff of the Italian Army, and because the treaty was secret, of course the people knew nothing. Meanwhile, the Neutralist opposition to war grew and the Government did little to stop the violence of the streets.

The emergence of Mussolini

Benito Mussolini was the editor of an Interventionist paper from Trent called 'Il Popolo d'Italia'. On 10th April 1915 he issued an unambiguous challenge: 'Seize the squares tomorrow, regardless of everything! No one can stop us! You are the law, you are the power!'* He appeared in Rome next day and after a speech in Piazza di Trevi he was arrested. On 4th May, the Italian Government denounced the Triple Alliance, i.e. with Germany and Austria. Then the 'glorious month of May' began. One demonstration followed another as though in rehearsal for the Fascist Era. A minority of violent men held the streets and squares. Gabriele D'Annunzio returned to Italy to celebrate the anniversary of the March of the Thousand under Garibaldi which had started on 5th May 1860 at the crag of Quarto, Genoa. He used the occasion to deliver an oration to incite Italy to war: 'Blessed are the young who hunger and thirst after glory, for they shall be satisfied'. The audience howled: 'Down with Austria!'

In Genoa that night there was a noisy demonstration outside the German consulate. Ricciotti Garibaldi appeared at the balcony of his hotel and delighted the crowd with 'War or revolution!'

That glorious month of May was a month of violent demonstrations and aggressive speeches. D'Annunzio stole the limelight from Mussolini, he was at the time a better stage manager! When he arrived in Rome, a crowd bearing torches escorted him along the Via Boncompagni. Later from the balcony of his hotel he addressed the crowd: 'Tonight we intend to counter cowardice with heroism! Let Italy take up arms, and not for an absurd parade, but for a bitter battle! Rome behold the challenge'. And he threw his white glove into the crowd.†

A few days later, on 13th May, it was rumoured that Salandra had been forced to resign. The crowds saw the

* ibid. p. 42.
† ibid. p.43.

prize of war snatched from their grasp, because it was known that Giolitti was still trying to avoid war. D'Annunzio spoke again: 'Hear me – heed me – treason is out in the open today . . . they seek to strangle our country with a Prussian rope.'*

Mussolini was not to be outdone. 'Il Popolo d'Italia' was his mouthpiece: 'Are we to believe that a few dozen miserable German politicians in Italy are capable of halting the course of our destiny with their intrigues?'† But Mussolini also harangued the crowds in Milan, a hostile demonstration was held outside the Archbishop's palace, stones were thrown and guns were fired. A mechanic named Luigi Gadda was killed and 18 wounded were taken to hospital. Mussolini threatened the King: 'We want war, and if you Sire, who under Article V of the Constitution can send all our soldiers to the frontiers, refuse us, you will lose your crown'.‡

When the rumour of Salandra's resignation was confirmed, uncontrollable violence broke out in the streets. His resignation had been handed in with the agreement of the King, who then refused to accept it. Parliament was put in turmoil and on 20th May it placed full power in the hands of the King. On 23rd May the King delivered an ultimatum to Austria, and on 24th May 1915 Italy went to war.

Active Service

King Victor Emmanuel III represented the war as a continuance of the war for the unification of Italy. The

* ibid..
† ibid..
‡ ibid. p.44.

'iniquitous' border accepted by Italy in 1866 was a constant source of irritation. Behind that line, in subjection to Austria lay 'unredeemed' or unliberated lands of Italian territory and Italian people. The Austrians did not enforce the use of German upon the Trentino, whose people remained fiercely Italian, although under Austrian rule. It was inevitable therefore that, when war was declared, the Italian armies should at once march into Austrian territory to reclaim their lands. They crossed on a broad front, meeting little resistance, from Brescia to Verona and Vicenza. The words of their King were to inspire them to continue the work of Garibaldi: 'To you, the glory to complete, at last, the work which your fathers began with such heroism!'*

Igino went first to Modena to attend the Academia Militare, to be prepared as an officer of the Italian army. At the end of his training, he was given five days leave to say goodbye to his family. We have learnt enough about this young man to realize the joy of that short home visit. He was a second lieutenant, in officer's uniform, and his family would be proud of him. He would have visited the church of S. Andrea, perhaps a meeting of the confraternity. I am sure he called on his old teachers and talked long with the priest.

The Italian troops advanced. The communiqué on the second day of the war announced the capture of Caporetto. By July, the Italians had crossed the Isonzo river and moved into Trentino. Igino after his brief leave was sent to the 11th Infantry Division on the Isonzo front. It was a mobile front, advancing and retreating, with the Austrians at first not putting their strong defences against the Italian advance. A kind of trench warfare developed and it became a fairly quiet front. But winter conditions

* ibid. p.46.

were terrible. The trenches were appalling. The Italian soldiers had inadequate protection against the weather and against the enemy. The wire cutters were unsuitable to cut through Austrian barbed wire and weapons were thoroughly out of date. The Italian army had been expanded in numbers, but not in equipment.

At first, apart from the misery of the weather in unhealthy trenches, the equipment did not matter too much. The allies were pressed on other fronts, especially in France, and men were needed from the Austrian Army elsewhere. The Austrians made no real thrust until January 1916. In that month, the Austro-Hungarian Armies under the spirited leadership of Marshal von Hötzendorf exploited a wedge they held in the Trentino and smashed through the Italian lines on two wide fronts.

Von Hötzendorf carried his forces deep into Italy, finishing along the line of the Val Lagarina and Valsugana, threatening the Veneto plain and the Italian armies on the Isonzo. The Austrians regarded the expedition as punitive, because these Italians, their ex-allies, had withdrawn from the Triple Alliance. It was a massive attack by two well equipped armies. By May 1916, the Italian line had broken and by June the Austrians had swept across the Altopiano and engulfed Asiago itself. An Italian counter-offensive was essential. Troops were drawn from the Isonzo front and Igino began the difficult journey to the Altopiano of Asiago. He commanded a platoon of men as a second lieutenant, but was soon promoted to first lieutenant. The conditions really were appalling and few thought they could survive in the mud and water and snow of the trenches. On the march, their tents were not even waterproof – perhaps a preparation for what they were going to have to endure in the trenches. They soon discovered how much the human frame can endure, and despite their poor equipment, they constituted a fine fighting force. They threw the Austrians back – at least part of the way. The front which had nearly reached Valsugana was thrown back to a line running from Corbin through Camporovere, Mt. Mosciag, Mt. Zerbio and as far as Mt. Ortogara. This was a line that could be defended and would protect Asiago and the whole Altopiano. But it left the Austrians in the high places and easily able to defend themselves against any further Italian advance. The Austro-Hungarian troops dug themselves in and were able to send forces to other war sectors. These high places would be costly to assault, but an attempt was made in an Italian counter-offensive, 25th to 27th June. At that point, the Italians had recovered about one third of the ground they had lost to the Austrians in their punitive expedition. After this Igino went with his company to Mt. Zerbio and then near to the fortress at Interrotto to Mt. Mosciag. All the time they were beneath Austrian positions. On Mt. Mosciag which they attempted to take during the 6–14th July offensive an event happened that put Lieutenant Igino Giordani out of the war and very nearly out of this life. A quote from his own notes about that incident, written many years later, will describe it best. The date was *7th July 1916:*

> One morning all the officers were gathered in a hut, when the Commander of the Army Corps (or Division) came with his whole entourage. He was a big name. He brought instructions from General Cadorna and told us that we had to assault the enemy and dislodge him, in a charge, absolutely in a charge . . . Offensive, not defensive warfare. Or else a counter attack – audacious, certain, immediate . . . His words were really quite impressive, for they brimmed with destructive force, to put it mildly, a Regal March: but up there no one was marching. We were rotting.
>
> As soon as the officers of the Army Corps left the

room, various officers of the Division (or Army Corps?) came in with another general. The new leader overturned the arguments and tactics of our previous colleague and recommended defensive, not offensive warfare. . .

In the end the only thing to do was to find some simple way of giving our superiors a demonstration that, on that front, it was tactically and strategically, logically and psychologically impossible to break through the defences and the embattled emplacements of our enemies. Having given this proof, everything would return to normal . . . The honour of the demonstration was to be mine, because I was the youngest officer. The captain explained to me that the general had chosen our company, and the commander of our company had chosen my platoon.

Before dawn my men, a group of twenty with me at their head, began climbing up to the Austrian defences, dragging behind us a canister of explosives that was to blow a hole through the mass of barbed wire. But the enemy spotted us immediately and opened fire. In just a few minutes, practically all the young men were either dead or wounded. With the help of a soldier (my batman) I managed to embed the canister of gelignite in the tangle of iron wire above our heads. It had to be detonated. While we were preparing the devices for this, I felt a knock (very soft, almost a flick) on my right leg, and immediately I saw it spin of its own accord and lift up again at random, on its own, as if it did not belong to me. I raised my right hand to stop it and glanced at my dangling fingers streaming with blood. I inferred that I was wounded.*

And he was – severely.

Out of the Battle

There was no doubt that the wounds were far more serious than anyone had realized at the time. His right leg

* *'Memorie'*, pp. 52–55.

had been shattered and the hand badly damaged. It was not a matter for the first-aid station, nor even for the military hospital just behind the lines. Although he did not know it at the time, there was little hope of saving the leg and only a slender hope of survival. The captain praised his gallantry and he was later decorated for those brave if rash actions of the 7th July. That was his last day of active service, although his promotion did not stop! In a series of hospitals during the remaining years of the war, he rose from Lieutenant to Captain, from Captain to Major and from Major to Lt. Colonel. It was a good war record if a brief one!

About the same time that Igino received his wound on Mt. Mosciag, a far more tragic event was taking place in Trent. There Lieutenant Cesare Battisti and second lieutenant Fabio Filzi were hanged as traitors in the moat of the old castle. Both were Italians, but natives of territory which had been under Austrian subjection. They both died on 12th July 1916 and their graves had a poignant meaning for Igino on his many visits to Trent when it was recovered for Italy.

Commenting on his rapid promotion in hospital, he said shyly: 'I could have become a general if the war had gone on a little longer. But sadly the pension remained that of a lieutenant!'

His war was over. With a shattered femur and a wounded hand, there was little chance that he would fight again. He was sent to Milan to the hospital of Baggina, where he was treated by a brilliant surgeon, Luigi Negri, under whose care his life and his leg were saved. There would be other hospitals and many more operations. In the following year he was moved to Rome to the temporary hospital in *Palazzo Margherita* where the US Embassy now is. In all, he was three years and some months in hospital.

The continuing war

Although Lieutenant Giordani had finished his war after only a year, the war continued, with its savage destruction of lives until 1918. As Italy's losses mounted, the poor leadership which is illustrated in Igino's story of the assault of Mt. Mosciag continued. The Italian soldiers were fine fighters and brave, but their equipment was faulty and their leadership poor.

In 1st August 1917, when losses on all fronts were reaching monstrous proportions, the Pope, Benedict XV, addressed his 'papal letter for peace' to all powers, describing the war as a needless massacre. Giolitti made his first speech since 1915, against war. Emissaries from Russia were greeted in Turin by 50,000 workers.

On 23rd August, insurrection broke out in Turin, Milan, Nice and other places. Barricades went up in the streets and there was nearly another Petrograd in Turin. A new dread began to fill the hearts of the 'ruling classes'. What would happen after the war? Italy had its successes and failures: General Capello's offensive on the Isonzo, but also the later loss of Caporetto. There were heroic gestures in the days of defeat.

Mussolini portrayed the tragic situation as the betrayal of the nation by Parliament: 'It is an appalling fact that 40 million Italians are nothing and 400 Deputies are everything!' What was to become his tone in later years was heard already in February 1918: 'I call for savage men. I call for a savage man who has strength, the strength to shatter, the inflexibility to punish, to strike without hesitation and the harder and oftener when the guilty are in high places' (Rome, 24th February 1918).★

★ Max Gallo, op. cit., p.53.

Meanwhile the war continued along the Piave – a hard war without pity. On 3rd November 1918, Italy struck its final blow and Austria signed an armistice next day in Padua. But the war had left its mark. In its dying moments it gave birth to Fascism.

3

The Hospital – University

Igino Giordani was fighting his own war for survival. The series of surgical operations which began at the Military Hospital at Baggina had to be undertaken with the most primitive form of anaesthetics.

The suffering was considerable. 'Religion helped me through month after month of suffering', he writes.* Some years later, Professor Negri confessed that he had had little hope of success. Most of those who had undergone similar operations under similar conditions had died. Giordani survived, but with considerably reduced strength, always in pain and unable to walk.

In the hospital ward, he was much encouraged by Sister Giuseppina, a nurse whose undaunted faith met the cynicism of many an officer. One particular extrovert atheist boasted that he had lost all faith. He marvelled that an intelligent girl like Giuseppina could believe all that talk of life after death. She answered him with a touch of his own mocking style: 'If I am mistaken, it is only for 10, 20, or 30 years; but if you are mistaken, it is for eternity'.†

During his long period in hospital Igino was relieved to receive a regular pension – if only a lieutenant's! It enabled him to have a few pleasures and to help his

* *'Memorie'*, p.57.
† ibid. p.58.

parents. A poor home like his needed all the support it could get. Quite incidentally he shows the poverty of the home in his description of the time in Tivoli when he waited with fear for the news that the Jesuits must go. He writes, 'For a month [around] . . . the pot of fire, full of glowing embers around which, in the middle of the kitchen, we kids gathered together with our grand-parents and neighbours . . .'* The picture of one centre of dying heat tells volumes about the poverty of that house, otherwise unheated in the midst of winter.

His war pension could be used also to help his mother and sisters now. Milan was a long way from Tivoli and he records with affection the visit of his father and mother. It was the first time they had left their immediate area for a journey longer than that to Rome. Even Igino did not see the sea until he joined the army! They knew little or nothing of trains and hotels, or distances for that matter, and so they made the long journey to Milan as best they could and when they had finished talking with their son, they just turned round and went home at once! It was probably this visit that made him seek permission to be moved closer to Tivoli. After ten months at Baggina, he was transferred to Rome.

The Queen's Hospital in Via Boncampagni

Igino Giordani came on a stretcher from Milan to Rome and was then placed in a villa of the Queen's Palace. This was the chosen home of the Queen Mother, Queen Margherita, after the assassination of her husband at Monza on 29th July 1900. She believed then in the pomp and ceremony of court, even though her son the new

ibid. p.29.

king, Victor Emmanuel III, chose an austere life, using the Quirinal Palace only as an office! The real pageantry of the monarchy was around Queen Margherita. The Villa Margherita was a vast residence with gardens and two villas as well as the main building – in every sense a palace.

Queen Margherita had followed the national aspirations of Italy with enthusiasm. She welcomed the Libyan War in 1911 and rejoiced that Italy would have a colony. The palace seemed to hum with activity as she took a hand personally in arranging emigration to the new colony. She was less enthusiastic about the entry into war in 1915 and foresaw a long and very hard war for Italy. She was, however, proud of her son, the King, who had set off for the front at once, and she devoted herself to the service of his country at war.

Carolina Marchi in her fascinating history of *'Palazzo Margherita'* describes how she made good use of her palace:

> She exploited the facilities of the spacious palace with its two villas and gardens to the maximum in the variety of relief work which she undertook . . . The two villas were immediately transformed into *Red Cross Territorial Hospital No.2.* The hospital included an operating theatre, 125 beds and the finest in modern surgical equipment. The military patients were provided with every comfort, from books and magazines to fresh flowers from the garden . . . From July 1915 until January 1919, this small but efficient hospital accommodated in all 687 military patients, and 600 operations were performed.*

Some of those operations were on Igino Giordani. He had spent 9 months in the hospital of Baggina in Milan and underwent continuous operations for a further 3 years in Rome.

*Carolina Marchi, *'Palazzo Margherita'*, De Luca, Rome, 1980, p.42.

These years were not lost. Igino intended to survive and to be a useful participant in the rebuilding of Italian life after the war. He learnt to play the violin and he studied as a 'home student'. He had always had an interest in archaeology and so that was his first subject. Among his earliest writings is a guide to two temples near Tivoli.* He retained his love of the classics and was able to have books sent to him in hospital. He studied history and sociology, wrote poems and developed an enthusiasm for Plato and Tacitus. Most of this work had to be done during a long convalescent stage, because in the earlier period of the operations he suffered unbearably. But both his violin playing and his studies progressed. Years later when he met Queen Margherita she remembered him – 'You are the one who was always studying', she said. He passed his first examination at the University as what we should call an 'external student' and then proceeded to graduate in Literature and Philosophy.

A girl from Tivoli

Wounded soldiers were visited by many grateful Italians, and as in other countries, there were girls who wrote to soldiers to cheer them. Igino received a letter from a *tiburtina*, a girl from Tivoli. Her letters moved him and he replied asking her to visit him. She would not because she was engaged and thought it was not proper to visit another man. She was the daughter of a middle-class family in Tivoli and although she could not visit she sent him a chain with a medal of the Madonna. He treasured it and thought often of her. Years later, he met her and found her in very poor circumstances. He had envisaged

*'*I templi di Vesta e della Sibilla in Tivoli*', Tip. Moderna, Tivoli, 1918.

her as beautiful and pure. That she had been, but by the time Igino saw her, she was deserted by her fiancé and badly in need of help. Igino was able to get her a job in order that she might be able to eat. She was alone without relatives or fiancé. 'Poor creature', Igino comments, 'she did not know how to live. She died in silence and misery, a humble and pure thing'.* There were others whom he remembered from those hospital years that lead us to believe that he was not always studying. His results were good. But he was also in love.

Engaged and married

Igino was in love with the woman he would eventually marry: Mya Ora-Finiamola Salvati. The second name was a little bizarre and possibly indicated a father's hope that she would be the last child. (*Ora finiamola* means 'Now let's finish!') If that is so, he was disappointed. Two sons were born to Mr. and Mrs. Salvati after Ora-finiamola! Her father was a lawyer and landowner. Mya was one of 12 children and had all the happiness of a large family. Igino was radiantly happy. He later described his fiancée as 'a delightful young woman, full of fun, enraptured by music, bursting with vitality and with a beautiful soprano voice'.

She was a girl of good middle-class family in Tivoli and there must have been the usual hesitations among the family as to whether it was a suitable marriage. Although an officer and well educated, he was from a poor family which would be well enough known in a town as small as Tivoli. But Igino quickly won everybody's heart. He soon proved himself able to support this girl of his love.

*'Memorie', p.60.

He had graduated in hospital and he obtained a post as teacher at the Umberto I Grammar School in Rome. A teacher, earning a salary, with an officer's pension, he was able to marry and he loved his job as a teacher. Mya's many brothers and sisters took him to their heart and there was every indication of a happy marriage.

The first home

On 2nd February 1920 they married and Igino found a flat in Via Cavour in Rome, where he took his bride after their honeymoon. The wedding was celebrated in a room of the Salvati household in Tivoli and both families seemed happy at the match. Their flat in Via Cavour was in the home of a Waldensian family with two children. Catholic and Waldensian have not always lived happily together, but Igino was able to recognize authentic faith, however much it differed from his own unwavering Catholicism. Igino Giordani never needed to oppose another's faith in order to establish his own. Within the family all was quiet and peaceful. But outside in the streets of Rome all was turmoil. The post-war years were driving Italy into the violence of Fascism and Giordani could hardly keep out of the struggle.

4

Postwar Politics

It was impossible for a man as sensitive and intelligent as Igino Giordani to fail to see the importance of politics. The incident of the expulsion of the Jesuits from Tivoli would have made him aware at an early age that political agitation could overthrow men of faith. His questioning during his years in the seminary and the state school must have raised the issue of Catholic involvement in politics. Perhaps the most powerful influence of all was the experience of war. The appeal of the Pope had not prevented entry into a ruinous war nor halted the meaningless massacre, but the Vatican and those devout Catholics who took their lead from the Pope found themselves politically isolated and powerless in all but domestic matters concerning the Church. 'Let the Church be the Church' had come to mean: 'Keep out of the political struggle'. And behind that was the implied accusation that Italy was not the *patria* of the Catholic Church.

Luigi Sturzo

This unsatisfactory situation was not accepted by all. The priest who led the Church out of political isolation and formed the party that would enable it to participate fully was *Don Sturzo*. His influence over Giordani was decisive.

He was much older, ordained a priest in the year that Igino was born. He was a Sicilian from Caltagirone, from a prosperous and noble family. Born 26th Nov. 1871, ordained a priest 19th May 1894, he studied philosophy and soon became deeply concerned with the poverty of the South (*Mezzogiorno*). He was frustrated by the discovery that the Church had so little political power to alleviate this poverty and the injustices of the social system. While quite young he argued for Catholic involvement with political problems. He was not satisfied with the separation of Church and State and opposed every effort to silence the Church on political issues. For years he struggled to bring Catholics, old and young, to a state of political consciousness. Speaking in his native Caltagirone, he put his position quite clearly:

> We Catholics are not simply to be attracted into the orbit first of the monarchists, then the conservatists, then the progressive socialists, but we are to remain, now and forever, necessarily democratic and catholic.★

He organized political structures at diocesan, parish and rural level throughout Sicily. In Noto and Caltagirone he prepared to stand as a Deputy in the Italian Parliament – the first priest to do so. And he won the seat. His political activity was inspired by Pope Leo XIII, whose encyclical, *'Rerum Novarum',* made this possible. Don Sturzo published a little book called 'The Cross of Constantine' which had a great influence in his campaign, and later upon Giordani.

The war years brought special tasks and opportunities. Catholic Action was formed in 1915 with the support of the compassionate Pope Benedict XV: Don Sturzo moved to Rome. Then when the war was over he set to

---

★ Luigi Sturzo, *'Discorso al circolo di lettura di Caltagirone',* 24th December 1905, in *'I discorsi politici',* Rome, 1951, p.379.

work on the problems of the post-war world. This, he said, was to be 'The new era of the people'.

On the evening of 17th January 1919, in a modest room of the *Albergo Santa Chiara*, by the bedside of the sick Don Sturzo, the formalities of establishing a new party, the *Partito Popolare Italiano* were carried through by the acceptance of its constitution. Today a plaque on the outside wall of the hotel marks the occasion, but the room is forgotten. Within a year huge white posters were to be seen in the major cities of Italy. At the top of each was the word *Libertas* (liberty), inscribed in a shield bearing a cross. This was to remain the emblem of the Italian Popular Party. Its posters printed its first manifesto:

> Inspired by the principles of Christianity that will hallow the great civilizing mission of Italy, [it called upon] all free, strong men to build a truly popular state.*

The party was the first organized expression in modern Italy of the Catholic Faith in political terms. There were many signatures, but the most prominent was that of the party's political secretary, Don Luigi Sturzo. He brought to that office the experience of mayor of Caltagirone and that of secretary general of Catholic Action. For him as for the Vatican, the goal was to make the Catholic masses definitively a factor in political life. In November 1918 he had an audience with the Vatican Secretary of State, in which Don Sturzo made it plain that he was not seeking to defend the privileges of the Church, nor to extend them, but to involve Catholics in responsible political action. He assured the Cardinal that he would do nothing antagonistic to the Church. Thus he was not seeking a Church party. Pope Benedict XV gave his consent and a wide range of Catholic support

* Translated from PPI Manifesto

followed. The Catholics were waiting for and ready for this party. It grew rapidly. As early as 1913, Giolitti, then Prime Minister, had come to an understanding with the Church, but this was the first political party in which Catholics could feel that they were supporting their own Christian values.

Il Partito Popolare Italiano

By common consent, the political event that dominated the beginning of 1919 was the constitution of the 'popular' party, the PPI, on 18th January 1919. The new party was the signal for the official entry of Italian Catholics into normal politics, after years of abstention, mitigated only by limited participation in the elections of 1904 and 1909, and even then only as an appendix to the Liberal Party. Through the energetic work of Don Luigi Sturzo, the new party had captured the trades union movement with its own Confederation of Italian Workers, supported by extensive Co-operatives. The Catholics had by 1921 no less than 311 co-operatives compared with the Socialist, 236. This popular tendency and organization of trades union, earned for the new party the name of 'white bolsheviks'.

Already in June 1919, the Popular Party had 56,000 enrolled members and was backed by 20 daily newspapers and 50 weeklies. The party was prepared for Italy's first election since the war. After a violent session of Parliament on 28th September 1919 in which Socialists and Fascists brawled, the King dissolved Parliament and the date of a new election was set for 16th November 1919. The PPI gained 100 seats.

Giordani's political involvement

The past months had seen much violence, but Giordani was at peace as he prepared for his wedding, although he was already politically concerned. When he married, the Popular Party was in Parliament with a good number of deputies and he had helped, writing and talking about the involvement of Catholics in politics. In his journeys to and from Rome and Tivoli, before his marriage, he had come into contact with Giuseppe Petrocchi, an educated man, employed at the Ministry of Information, who was writing a profile of Don Sturzo. Seeing that Giordani was interested, he arranged for them to meet. This led to an involvement in the weekly journal of the party called 'Il Popolo Nuovo'. He was soon active every day in the little office in Via Ripetta, which at that time was very modest, employing four people: a priest, Don Giulio De Rossi, Spataro, Scelba, and Igino Giordani. A few members of the party also gave a hand when things were busy. Giordani soon had to give up teaching, because of the work which a growing party involved. He became a disciple of Don Sturzo who was much attached to him. They walked together each day for exercise, and to discuss books and politics, from via Ripetta, along the bank of the Tiber, to *Ponte del Risorgimento* and back along the other bank. It was on one of these walks that Don Sturzo asked him to stand as a Deputy in 1921. The party was then the second largest in Parliament.

Much to the surprise of the Fascists and the Conservatives, the results of the 1919 elections had been: Socialists, 1,840,593; Popular Party, 1,175,000 votes. There were now 156 Socialist deputies instead of 51; and 102 deputies from the Popular Party. Two new blocs had been created seizing the majority of the seats from the old parties. Don Sturzo had altered the shape of the Italian Parliament.

The Manifesto of the PPI

Igino Giordani had found a cause and a political party which he could whole-heartedly support. On the 18th January 1919, following that evening meeting of the 'provisional committee', the PPI had issued an appeal to all 'free, strong men' and called upon them to create a 'truly popular state'; and the posters had clearly stated that this party was to be 'inspired by the principles of Christianity'. These words were not mere rhetoric. Attached to the appeal was a programme, which so long as it could, the PPI attempted to put into practice.

The programme had 12 points:

1. Defence of the family against all forms of dissolution and corruption.

2. Popular education and war against illiteracy.

3. Recognition and representation of trades union at all levels of public work, parish, district and national.

4. National and international legislation to guarantee the rights of the worker.

5. National programmes for the development of energy and industry, with special concern for the national responsibility to develop the agriculture of the *Mezzogiorno*.

6. The recognition of the rights of local government and freedom to develop local initiative. With this goes a reform of bureaucracy and slow decentralization of administration towards cooperation.

7. Reorganization and development of public assistance.

8. Freedom and independence of the Church, with liberty and respect for the Christian conscience, 'considered as foundation and defence of the life of the nation, the liberty of the people and the spread of civilization throughout the world.'

9. Reform of local and national fiscal systems on the

basis of a progressive tax with exemption at the level of lowest income.

10. Electoral reform with proportional representation and votes for women.

11. National defence. Protection and control of Italian emigration. Colonial policy of education and of industrial development in accordance with national interests.

12. Support for the League of Nations.★

The control of the streets

In Italy feelings ran high: Mussolini and his Fascists were showing already their power to control the streets and there was continuing dissatisfaction with the way in which the Allies had robbed Italy, as she thought, of her fruits of victory.

At the age of 78, Giovanni Giolitti had been returned to power. There was not enough in common between him and Don Sturzo to form a coalition. The Fascists had only a small band of members in Parliament, but they soon held the streets. As in Germany later, it was a battle between the Communists and the Fascists. Again, as in Germany, the devaluing of the currency undermined confidence in the government.

On 24th June 1920, the very day when Giolitti was to present his programme, the Royal Guard was firing on the crowds in Milan and Piombino and a general strike was called in the province of Belluno. There appeared to be a military rising and disturbance flowed over from

★ Giuseppe Bonfanti, 'Documenti e Testimonianze di Storia Contemporanea', Vol.2, 'Il Fascismo – 1. la conquista del potere', La Scuola, p.55f., selected from the full text.

Umbria to Rome. The army mutinied in Ancona, insurrection spread from the barracks to the city and then to the towns of Forli and Pesaro. The government was not powerless, but threatened. The Socialist Party with its various organizations had a membership of 2,150,000; while the Popular Party had allied to it the Italian Workers Federation (CIL) together numbering 1,161,238. But the strength was potential rather than dynamic.

One could imagine the hopes in the office of the Popular Party where Giordani was now working when, in the municipal elections of 31st October and 7th November 1920, the PPI won control of 1,613 communes. The support for a party standing for a Christian Democracy seemed to be growing. But there were other forces than the ballot box.

The disillusionment of the post-war recession, the stirring calls of D'Annunzio, like some modern-day Don Quixote, encouraged the brutal assertions and violent action of the Fascists. Mussolini had already given notice that he had other ways to power than the ballot box. Dino Grandi, the Fascist leader in Bologna, was to say in November 1920: 'The elections were held between two punitive expeditions. For the Fascists they were no more and no less than an incident in their civil war. The election campaign was carried on without a programme; it was simply an *anti-Socialist* campaign'.*

Assassination, terrorism and violence marked the campaign. But the results were remarkable and by no means the verdict of a frightened electorate: the Socialists retained 122 seats, the Communists won 16 and the Popular Party increased its representation from 102 to 107. Mussolini came to Parliament at the head of 35

* Max Gallo, op. cit., p.120.

Fascists. The newspaper 'L'Avanti' was premature in declaring: 'The Italian proletariat has swamped Fascist reaction under an ocean of red ballots'. One should rather have heeded Mussolini's cryptic comment: 'We will not be a parliamentary group but an assault squad and a firing squad'.

The power of the pen

Igino Giordani saw post-war Italy, which he had antici-pated so differently, in the comparative serenity of school, the trenches, the hospital, becoming a nation of boastings and threats, in which those who had profited from the war turned their polemics against those who had suffered from it. He had already written many articles and now his pen turned angry. 'My anger was converted into a violent and vivid prose', he noted many years later. One of the most furious of his articles was at the assassination of Giacomo Matteotti on June 10th 1924.★ Giordani knew that he was in dangerous water. Opposition to Fascism was usually met with a bullet and his article had been outspoken and angry. Everyone knew that the Fascists had killed Matteotti. It took courage to say so publicly.

The Fascist regime silenced the Holy See by threaten-ing to attack all Catholic organizations, and with no protection from the Church, Don Sturzo wisely began his long exile abroad. Before he left he gave Giordani this piece of advice: 'Learn English'. Giordani already knew a few phrases and he now set to work in earnest, buying, as he records, a book called 'English in 11 lessons'. Don

★ *'Rivolta Cattolica'*, Gobetti, Turin, 1925; Colletti, Rome, 1945; Lice, Padua, 1962.

Sturzo kept up a regular correspondence with him which later he published (1969).

With Don Sturzo in England and later in America, the Popular Party needed a new leader in Italy. On 19th May 1924, the National Council of the PPI unanimously agreed to offer the position of political secretary to De Gasperi. He accepted and moved from Trent to Rome. Thus Giordani and De Gasperi had daily contact in the Via Ripetta. This became particularly close as Mussolini turned his attack upon De Gasperi.

The main organ of attack was the newspaper 'Il Popolo d'Italia' for which Mussolini's brother Arnaldo wrote. De Gasperi personified the idea of Democracy, which was the enemy of Fascism, and most serious of all he had in the PPI the best organized political force in Italy. He led it wisely. The attack by 'Il Popolo d'Italia' was abusive and set the tone of much Fascist propaganda. It was a slander campaign seeking to discredit De Gasperi. By the autumn of 1924 it had reached its climax and a defence had to be made. De Gasperi wrote the material for the defence but persuaded Giordani to publish it as his. Actually, the inflammatory preface was written by Giordani. It was powerful rhetoric and convincing in its sincerity, but De Gasperi was more anxious to let the facts speak for themselves. His letter to Giordani was also printed because its plain sincerity would make a great appeal. In that letter, De Gasperi asked Giordani to leave aside all comments and let the facts and testimony speak their own language of serenity and objective documentation. He asked Giordani not to make too high a claim for what he had accomplished. Most of the charges had been made about De Gasperi's work in Trentino and he was anxious that all should recognize that his own achievements, which Giordani might be tempted to exaggerate, could only be seen in the setting of the efforts made by the people of the Trentino. 'If there is to be praise let it be for the Trentino people who have always had their political, economic and social leaders and in the hour of trial their martyrs and heroes! De Gasperi ended this letter with:

> I know that I have been only a humble servant of a great cause, my only desire for my defence is that the good faith and truth of this cause be made known, a cause which I have always tried to serve with dignity, sincerity and unselfishness.★

The political style of Giordani: the defence of De Gasperi

After that letter, Igino Giordani placed his *Introduction*. It contrasted in style with that of De Gasperi. At once he saw and said that the campaign in 'Il Popolo d'Italia' was launched as part of a systematic method which was soon to become common as Fascism grew in strength and confidence. The style was necessary for the defence of such a regime. It had to crush the protest of the national conscience against the political crime of Fascism. It could do this only by slandering the head of its parliamentary opposition. In the eyes of the regime: 'De Gasperi had but one unpardonable crime – his leadership of the strongest opposition party'. We have a very good example of Giordani's style in the Introduction. It is penetrating, accurate and mocking. His opponents learnt to fear his rhetoric. But this was 1925 when Igino Giordani was not yet much more than 30. Let me quote from this Introduction to *'La verità storica e una campagna di denigrazione'* (The true story and a campaign of denigration):

★ *'La verità storica e una compagna di denigrazione contro Alcide De Gasperi'*, Arti Grafiche tridentine, Trent, 1925 (reprinted 1953).

If Mr De Gasperi, instead of being the leader of the PPI had been a pillar of the regime, the Fascist newspapers would have had nothing against him. They would have covered him with honours . . . The honourableness of a man consists in how much and when he serves the regime. At the first hint of criticism or protest, however legitimate, all of a sudden he becomes the quintessence of the qualities opposed to those that had been conferred upon him a moment before. Everything must be understood in the context of this . . . historical criticism of hosanna and crucifiction, which, apart from anything else, corresponds to the logic and praxis of Fascist thought, and which admits of only two kinds of citizens: the card-carrying members of the Fascist Party (assorted patriots, exclusively national, righteous, strong, honourable, and so on and so forth) and the card-carrying members of other parties (all labled antipatriots, guaranteed anti-nationals, unrighteous, cowardly, ignoble, and so on and on and on). Put, then, in the context of this never yet denied mentality, the episode of the campaign against Mr De Gasperi cannot but be seen as an organic discharge of slander, erupting exclusively from the subjective psychological foundation of incorruptible party feeling.

Such slander does not deserve to be refuted or replied to. But since it does provide a practical example of the Fascist method of denigration, it is useful in order to clarify its terms and techniques. At the same time it offers a welcome opportunity to highlight, however inadequately, the patriotic fervour of those thirty Catholics from the region of Trent who, under foreign domination during the war, put into effect such admirable resistance, understanding it as their civic duty and not waving it about like a flag to be appropriated for political points.*

De Gasperi had been accused of pro-Austrian sympathies during the war. This was part of an attack upon the devout Catholics of the Trentino.

Giordani ends this Introduction with an appeal to all

* ibid. p. 11f..

members of the PPI to rally behind their leader with a more intense solidarity. He points out that the pamphlet is largely documentary. It demonstrates, in his words, 'two things: the moral wretchedness of the slanderers and the civic virtues of the leader of the Popular Party'.

The first part of the pamphlet documents the activities of De Gasperi before and during the war; the second part takes up point by point the slander and intimidation, meeting even the smallest accusation with a clear refutation. It was sent to all involved in politics. The majority did not answer, largely out of fear for the consequences of getting involved. Among those who did support Giordani and answered with thanks were Giustino Fortunato and Carlo Sforza.

Catholic Action

The *Partito Popolare Italiano* was not a Church party, but it had agreed to do nothing antagonistic to the Church. Thus many devout Catholic laypeople were attracted to a party which stood for Christian values. But what of the Church itself? How far did it encourage its laypeople to take responsible action in the political world?

For most of Giordani's life the laity had been seen as little more than adjuncts to the clergy, assisting them to carry out their apostolic task. After the First World War there was an increasing realization that the laity had a special influence to exercise, an influence which only they could exert in their capacity as laymen and women. The lead came from Pius XI who already as Archbishop of Milan had supported Catholic Action. He recommended that lay movements in other countries should be studied and imitated. He was elected Pope in 1922. His influence was considerable and Igino Giordani could operate in a more favourable atmosphere than many before him. What Pius XI wanted to see was a band of militant laymen and women operating under the auspices of the hierarchy in every country. He wanted these laypeople to take their stand on religious grounds and rally the faithful under the banner of Christ as universal king, to work for the reintroduction of Christian standards into private and public life at both the national and international level. It was this integrated Catholic Action that he regarded as 'the apple of his eye'.

The laypeople were recognized even though they still seemed to be like second class citizens of the Church. Pius XI came to be known as the 'Pope of Catholic Action' and there were times when he seemed to have a vision for the laity which the structures of the Church found difficult. Writing to Cardinal Segura in 1929 he says that Catholic Action 'is nothing less than the apostolate of the faithful who, under the direction of their bishops, lend their aid to the Church of God and in a fashion complete her pastoral ministry'. National government also found this idea of a Catholic organized influence difficult and Pius XI made every effort to guarantee the security of branches of Catholic Action in different countries with clauses in its many concordats. In 1931, for example, he made it clear to the Fascist Government that he would tolerate no infringement of the rights of the Italian Catholic Action. The form of this organized lay apostolate varied from country to country.

In Belgium, for example, the developing trend towards 'specialized Catholic Action' was able to revitalize an earlier vision of banding young Catholic workers together. Although this vision goes back to 1913, it was not possible until 1925 when the Abbé, later Canon, Cardijn, launched the *Jeunesse Ouvrière Chrétien* (JOC). The JOC left its mark on Catholic Action and changed the image of many a parish. The industrial workers, and the young at that, were now mobilized into the lay apostolate. The structures of the Church were against it and the hopes which Pius XI and the promotors entertained for Catholic Action found only modest fulfilment. However, it was in Catholic Action that Chiara Lubich found her first opportunities and the subsequent Focolare Movement owes much to these early stirrings among the laity of the Church. In a sense, Igino Giordani was being prepared for later fulfilment through the Focolare by this early recognition of the place of the laity.

There is no doubt that but for the growth of Catholic Action in many countries of Europe, laypeople in the Catholic Church would not have made the enormous contribution they did in the post-war years and throughout the period of totalitarian rule in many countries. It could be that political frustration would have led many to abandon the Church if they had not found some activity for their political conscience. The Communists in every country are always ready to receive these politically conscious Catholics who have become impatient with their secondary role in the Church.

But Catholic Action made slow progress. The reasons are important for the development of Giordani. They include deliberate obstruction in totalitarian countries, where the timid Church leaders often restrained the eager laity. This led to an increasing tendency of Catholics to retreat into their shells and concentrate on the recovery of the lapsed rather than the conquest of the world. But when all is said, the failure of Catholic Action was more due to the apathy of the faithful who would rather not be disturbed. There was no apathy about Giordani and he was prepared to have his office become a 'centre of conquest'.

He faced two difficulties: the tendency of many

Catholics to prefer individualistic religion, which meant a high standard of private morality with little application of religious principles to public and political affairs, *and* the reluctance of the priests to allow the laity to proceed at too quick a pace. Catholic Action stimulated the political responsibility of devout Catholics and provided structures for activity, but it did not go far or fast enough. It was the political parties which had to carry the burden of putting Christian principles into action in the world of politics. And these parties were now threatened by Fascism.

5

Fascism

In the inter-war years, Liberal Democracy was challenged throughout Europe. Apart from the old pattern of resistance to democratization of feudal societies which was evident in eastern Europe, the Balkans, Spain, Portugal and Austria, there was the more serious threat of Fascism. The ideas of Liberal Democracy rested upon the acceptance of the essential worth and dignity of the individual, whose welfare was the *raison d'etre* of the state; by definition the state was the servant of the individual not the master. Liberal Democracy assumed that people were rational and could act responsibly so that the state could be trusted to their judgement. This meant certain essential institutions – legal guarantees of individual rights against arbitary actions by other individuals or even the state itself, including the right to hold and express opinions and to form voluntary groups. It meant acceptance by the minority of majority rule and respect by the majority of minority rights.

Fascism denied these basic assumptions about man – his rationality, his potentiality for responsible action and his basic value as an individual. It denied that the essential purpose of the state was to secure the freedom and welfare of the individual. It asserted the value of the state as an end in itself. Far from trusting the judgement and capacity of the people, Fascism exalted the leadership principle and made irrational loyalty a substitute for rational choice. On these premises the Fascist states scorned and suppressed democratic institutions – parliamentary forms, party organizations as a means of expressing diversity of opinion, and many of those personal freedoms which the liberal states guaranteed. Support for Fascism came partly as a result of the failure of the Liberal Democracies to deal with the economic decline subsequent upon the depression of the twenties.

Catholic resistance

Catholic resistance to Fascism was hampered from the beginning. The Church had supported feudal states in Spain, Portugal and Austria. It had failed to enter fully into political responsibility in the Democratic states, sometimes because of its minority status and the struggle for its own recognition – as for example in England where Catholic rights to be treated as full citizens occupied the attention of many Catholics who would otherwise have played a part in political activities. Italy was a crucial country and we have seen how for most of Giordani's early life Catholics were kept out of politics. When Don Sturzo led the Catholics out of their isolation, Fascism was already growing. The *Democrazia Cristiana* (DC) which eventually emerged had to fight on two fronts, against threats to Liberal Democracy from the right (Fascism) and to Christianity from the left (Communism).

Mussolini had already taken power in Rome in 1922 and the rigged elections of 1924 gave him a majority. The assassination of Giacomo Matteoti on 10th June 1924 showed what would happen to any who claimed the right to utter critical opinions. Igino Giordani was not diplomatic in his writing. We have referred already to the courage of the article in which he accused the Fascists of assassinating Matteoti – not as an isolated act, but 'In consequence of their principles'. His articles, both in 'Popolo' under the editorship of Donati, and in 'Popolo Nuovo', caused such a stir and were so obviously the spearhead of the Catholic attack on Fascism that Piero Gobetti asked him to collect them together in a book.*

Piero Gobetti

Apart from the great reputation of this young writer and poet, Piero Gobetti was becoming the symbol of resistance to Fascism. He did not hesitate to speak out, and he undermined many of the appeals for support which the Fascists relied upon. Eventually he was assassinated in Paris on 15th February 1926. Giordani was keeping dangerous, but honourable company, and some of his articles in this collection, which he called *'Rivolta Cattolica'* were direct attacks upon the principles of Fascism as we shall see. Of course, the book was quickly banned by the Fascists, but not before Piero Gobetti had edited it and published it in Torino in 1925. Further attempts to bring it out in 1943 and 1945 failed and ultimately it was published in its finished edition only in the safety of 1962. That, First Edition, as it is called in its new form, carries an introduction which shows Giordani's high regard for Piero Gobetti:

> In 1924 Piero Gobetti – who seemed to me like an adolescent with the eyes of a poet, fascinated by philosophy – invited me to collect some of my articles and compile them in a volume for his publishing house. I did this gladly, knowing who Gobetti was. He gave me full

* *'Rivolta Cattolica'*, op. cit..

freedom, and the book with the title 'Rivolta Cattolica' was successful and managed to encourage a few anti-fascist Catholics.*

Only a few months after the publication, Piero Gobetti was dead, killed by those whom Giordani opposed in this collection.

'Rivolta Cattolica'

Before we come to examine this major collection of Igino Giordani's early articles, we need to recall that he was a sensitive, religious intellectual before his pen was dipped deeply into the political ink of his day. He was a devout Catholic, but able to question his Church and show some dissatisfaction with the way in which the laity was not allowed to develop. He wanted faithful laymen and women to play their part in the conquest of the world for Christ. He had the energies of youth. He had already studied the ancient history of Rome; he had also studied the Church Fathers; he had published a book on Tertullian and one on Justin Martyr.† He was already a serious writer and author. He had some experience of teaching and of administration. His passion for social justice was noticed by Don Sturzo and he had political experience. This was no young hopeful whom Piero Gobetti asked to produce a book of articles which, clearer than any other I know, shows the Catholic resistance to Fascism in white heat.

The first section of the book is called 'War and Post War'. It has a dedication taken from the Old Testament:

---

* ibid. p.9.

† 'Preliminari d'apologetica cristiana', Rivista di cultura, Rome, 1923.

For out of Zion shall go forth the law,
and the word of God from Jerusalem.
He shall judge between the nations,
and shall decide for many peoples;
and they shall beat their swords into ploughshares,
and their spears into pruning hooks;
Nation shall not lift up sword against nation,
neither shall they learn war any more. *

The articles in this first section are mostly anti-militarist and an appeal for trust in the power of the spirit rather than bayonets. They are written by one who has known war with its futility and has no desire to see a whole new generation brought up to glorify war or be sacrificed to it. There is an article on 'The Law of Nations' dated 25th September 1921 which begins typically: 'It is the custom to speak ill of the League of Nations. I will therefore speak well of it!'† He does, not claiming much, but he argues that with all its imperfections, the League offers an opportunity for an alternative to fratricidal war. If the press would cease from lampooning it or the bourgeoisie recognize the need for it, then it could bring great rewards – an international law, arbitration between the nations by reason rather than force, etc. His words were wise and incisive, but they were not popular in an Italy which had recently won a war, although at a terrible cost. In the copy of *'Rivolta Cattolica'* which Igino gave me he listed a number of articles for my special attention. Most of these dealt with a dynamic form of Catholicism which called for social responsibility. They could almost have been 'Catholic Action' pamphlets. But what surprised me most was the extent to which he had anticipated so much in the Focolare Movement. This was a piety, completely

* Isaiah 2:3–4.
† *'Rivolta Cattolica'*, op. cit., p.32f..

orthodox, even when critical of the official line. It sprang from a devotion to the Church and to Christ. In the twenties, Igino was seeing clearly the dangers of the Italian state, both politically from the irresponsible leaders of thought and morally from the creeping paganism of the land. There was one reference which he had underlined and I shall summarize this. It is entitled, 'Disagreement with Papini' and was written for 'Il Popolo Veneto' on 18th February 1923.*

In an interview, Papini had said: 'The fundamental problem of our time is not political but moral. The real need is to live better lives and to raise the moral tone of life in society'. And Giordani retorts:

> Well then, it seems to me that all genuine Catholics would agree with that. Such, despite working in different fields, are for instance Papini and Meda, Fr Semeria and Don Sturzo, who, above all, clearly has the rarest political temperament, the most faithful to all that Catholic tradition has put forward in Italy for 59 years, from the first attempt at reintegration in the national life, to the formulation and development of Christian-Democratic principles into an organic political, economic, administrative, fiscal, social system, firm within a Christian moral structure.†

Giordani then quotes Don Sturzo, from an address he gave in Florence in January 1922. It can be taken to be Giordani's view at the time:

> We prefer the method of lawful resistance and bringing out the value of spiritual directions: not only because we believe this is the only possible way for us, but also because it corresponds to our ethical convictions and our religious vision. We have never confused religion with civil, political or economic institutions . . . but we cannot escape the ethical problems of life, nor their social

* ibid. pp. 106–109
† ibid. p.107.

implications or their moral strength . . . By transposing the moral implications of Christianity into the field of political and economic activities, the members of the PPI have taken the step which excludes the illegitimate use of violence, whether individual or collective. And in such a programme they have a conception of popular moral values which reaches back through two thousand years of Christian tradition. And even in politics we give the greatest consideration to moral values which must be aimed at giving also in political and public life a strength of character which today is sought in vain. And this is a side neglected by all other parties, who are bound to a materialistic view, but which is instead the main and most profound principle of the *risorgimento* of our people, who have still enormous moral reserves in the family and in religion, which are true forces for the expansion of our life in work and in economics. . . *

Throughout this article, Giordani shows his resistance to violence and he constantly recalls the horrors of the battlefields so recent in men's memories. He echoes Don Sturzo in appealing for a use of the true resources of the Italian people in their thousand years of Christian tradition rather than the dependence upon armies.

Giordani's teachers

One section towards the end of *'Rivolta Cattolica'* is a series of studies of outstanding figures who had influenced Igino Giordani in his earlier years.† The section is called *Maestri nostri* (our teachers).

This series of short studies is not only of people whom he followed, but clearly at this stage, when he was in his early thirties, these are the people whom he was not able to ignore.

* ibid..
† ibid. pp. 261-304

St. Catherine of Siena. The involvement of St. Catherine in the political life of the 14th century had made her a guide for the devout Catholics in politics. He saw in this daughter of a Sienese dyer, who wrote to kings, popes and governments, in the 'precious blood of Jesus', the example of a spirituality that embraced politics. In all the schisms and political upheaval of her day she took part with spirituality unstained. Her fine intelligence and indomitable courage were wholly dedicated to the service of 'the sweet First Truth', as she called Jesus. It was largely due to her efforts that the Holy See returned to Rome from Avignon in 1376. After outlining her incredible activity Giordani exclaims – 'St. Catherine died at 33!' which was not so far from his age at the time. She was his answer to those who said the priest and the devout Catholic should keep out of politics.

Windthorst and Bismarck. A strange pair, but clearly Giordani's sympathies were more with Ludwig Windthorst, the Catholic politician and leader of the *Centrum* party in Germany, who while not always in agreement with Rome, maintained the Catholic position in the German cultural struggle against Bismarck. Giordani's interest in Bismarck was largely due to his treatment of the 'national Catholics'. The contrast is brought out well by a terse comment: 'Windthorst is dead, but lives; Bismarck lives, but is dead'.★

Lacordaire and Montalembert. The priest and the layman, who had done for 19th century France what Don Sturzo and Giordani were aiming at in 20th century Italy. Father Lacordaire had called upon the Church to renounce its priviliges and accept the same kind of liberty as other citizens. He accepted the disappearance of the *Ancien Régime*. The proper place for the Church in politics, he

★ ibid. p.271.

saw as liberal, not defending priviliges. His position was very close to that of the PPI later. Montalembert was the devout Catholic layman, a liberal also in politics. Giordani had already compiled an anthology of his writings.

Tommaseo. A figure from the heroic period of the Italian *Risorgimento,* a friend of Alessandro Manzoni. Giordani admired the way in which Nicolo Tommaseo accepted Catholicism in its dogmatic integrity – unlike Mazzini, who invented a religion of his own, and Gioberti, who interpreted Catholicism idealistically.

Sturzo. Enough has been said already to show the influence of Don Luigi Sturzo. The essay is important for an assessment of how Giordani himself at this early period saw the strength of Don Sturzo's political philosophy. It ends with: 'The Fascists have a hundred and one reasons for hating Luigi Sturzo'.*

Don Giulio De Rossi. The obituary of a contemporary, who was his colleague in the PPI. Giordani admired the simplicity of the man, despite his brilliance and obvious importance. The obituary opens: 'Don Giulio is dead. That is how we knew him: Don Giulio. The young Catholics, the poor from the inner city, the journalists and politicians, the scholars and those living in the so-called subversive quarters of Rome, all called him simply that.'†

From all these he learnt, but from none more than from Don Luigi Sturzo, unless it be St. Catherine of Siena.

* ibid. p.300.
† ibid. p.301.

Piazza Santa Chiara

There is a little square in Rome with two plaques which bring together these two major influences upon Igino Giordani. The one, already mentioned, is on the wall of the *Albergo Santa Chiara*. It simply records that in one of the rooms of that hotel, the PPI was formed and that from the meeting around the bedside of the ailing Don Sturzo, an appeal to all free men and strong was sent out on 18th January 1919.

A few feet away, there is another plaque that Saint Catherine of Siena died near that spot on 29 April 1380. This second plaque was erected in 1980, the sixth centenary of her tragic death at the age of 33. It was the failure to solve the Great Schism in the Roman Church which less than two years before had brought her exhausted and broken-hearted to Rome to die. She was canonized in 1461 and much later declared a Doctor of the Church by Pope Paul VI in 1970.

In that little square, just off the more famous Piazza Navona, a short walk from the offices of *Centro Uno*, where 'Foco' served the ecumenical work of the Focolare Movement so faithfully, the two major influences in his early life and thought are recorded.

6

The Librarian

Such a man could not last long in Fascist Italy. He survived the first two phases of Fascism, but by 1925, after Mussolini had virtually closed the Chamber of Deputies, it was only a matter of time before Igino Giordani would be disposed of. He had been critical of the *Federazione Arditi d'Italia*, that death squad of intrepid fighters which had been formed during the war and became part of Mussolini's force for revolution.* Many of the articles in '*Rivolta Cattolica*' had been published in that first phase of Fascism, but the more critical articles were published in the second phase, between the march on Rome (28th October 1922) and the speech by Mussolini in the Chamber on 3rd January 1925. During this period, Mussolini had tried to act more or less constitutionally. But even in that period, Matteotti, who denounced the Fascist use of violence and intimidation in the Chamber, was murdered. Giordani had not hesitated to lay the blame on the *arditi*. Don Luigi Sturzo had been forced into voluntary exile, from which it soon became evident that he would not return. The virulent attacks on Alcide De Gasperi had been met by a publication appearing over the signature of Igino Giordani. Once Mussolini had declared himself dictator, there was no place for Giordani in politics or journalism.

* Giuseppe Bonfanti, op. cit., p.13.

The schoolteacher

Giordani could not live on a war pension and support his wife. And a child was expected. He had to find other work. The natural step was to return to teaching. In the state school that would have been impossible, but he secured a post in a church school, *Instituto Cabrini*, in Rome. It was a girls' school, run by a Mother Saverio of the Mission of the Sacred Heart. Igino describes her as a shrewd woman, energetic and fundamentally good. The appointment was for the school year, 1926-1927. The salary was low, but Igino managed to supplement it by giving private tuition. In 1926, his first son, Mario, was born.

Meanwhile some of his friends, including Cardinal Lucidi worked to obtain him a post in the *Biblioteca Vaticana*. It was in connection with this that he received an invitation to join a party to visit the USA and there study librarianship in preparation for a complete revision of the cataloguing system of the Vatican Library. The four chosen for this trip were: Mgr. Enrico Benedetti, Father Carmelo Scalia, Professor Gerardo Bruni and Professor Igino Giordani. The American newspaper cutting, under the heading of 'Catholic Scholars in the United States for Ideas', describes all four as 'members of the staff of the Vatican Library' and explains that they have come to study the organization and administration of American libraries. Mgr. Benedetti and Father Scalia, it explains will spend several weeks in the Library of Congress, Washington D.C., while Professors Bruni and Giordani 'will visit private libraries in New York, Boston and Ann Arbor, Mich.'

The New World

The party of four took the train to Le Havre then embarked on the liner 'Paris' to New York, where they disembarked on 31st August 1927. After a short stay in New York, Gerardo Bruni and Igino Giordani went to attend a course in library science at Ann Arbor, arranged by the University of Michigan. A semester there and then back to New York for a more advanced course with a further term at Columbia University.

Igino Giordani made many friends in the USA and he greatly broadened his views. It was there that he met the Protestant Churches in their natural setting. In Italy, his views of Protestantism were inevitably narrow and limited. They were often coloured by those priests who had left the Catholic Church to become hostile to it in an agressive form of Protestantism. Of course, he also met in America a number of anti-Catholic views, but the hostility was of a different kind. His own up-bringing too had been narrow so far as the Protestants were concerned although he must have learnt much from his first home with the Waldensians. But this did not prepare him for what he found in America, where there were large flourishing Churches which were not sects.

He also met racism. To his annoyance, he found the Italians were classified in much the same way as negroes, Chinese, Jews or Puerto Ricans. As he was in America at the time of the Depression, it was hardly surprising that he was shocked by what he called 'the hegemony of the dollar'. But his mind was mostly on his work and his notes do not contain much of social assessment. His visits to libraries were the best part of his time, sparking off ideas about what he would do back in the Vatican Library. In Detroit, Washington (largely the Library of Congress), Chicago, Philadelphia, he discovered American authors and even compiled an anthology of American writing, which later he published in translation.* He kept the feast of St. Catherine of Siena, 29th April 1928, by professing his vows next day in the Church of St. Vincent Ferreri, New York, as a tertiary in the Dominican Order.

An 'English' Diary

During his time in America, Igino practised his English by writing his diary up in this new language. Rereading it years later, he said: 'I recapture a little of the impressions that were so vivid to me and the preoccupation with the newness of it all, the pain of a certain resistance to the Italians which shocked me. But above all the diary reminds me of my major preoccupation with money, my family (wife and Mario) without enough to live on'.† There was clearly not enough to spare from the student stipend and his writings for Italian journals are mentioned in the diary – 'Avvenire d'Italia', 'Carroccio', etc. He tells us that he also wrote for 'Commonweal', whose editor Michael Williams later became a great friend. An entry in the diary for 11th February gives the cost of his food: 'breakfast, 15c; lunch, 50c; supper, 20c' and he adds 'subway, 20c'. He was obviously managing his limited resources carefully.

A week later, we find, breakfast, 9c, rent for the room at Columbia University, $1.45, lunch, 20c, a watch for his wife, $5.

Giordani embarked on the S.S. New Amsterdam, 26th May 1928, and he notes that the fare of $155 was reduced for students to $105.

* *'Contemporanei nordamericani'*, SEI, Turin, 1930
† *'Memorie'*, p.78f..

On his way home, he called at Paris and met several leading Catholic writers. Two he mentions in particular:* *Giovanni Rossi* was a charismatic character and there was much in him to fascinate the young Giordani. He founded the Paulist Fathers and an organization called the *'Cardinal Ferrari'*. Soon afterwards it moved to Assisi, where in the 30's a lay Movement, *'Pro Civitate Christiana'*, was started. Distinguished people from the Italian political and cultural world took part in it and, like its leader, it made an impression on Giordani.

Giuseppe Prezzolini, who was the other name he mentioned, was quite a different man. His long contacts with the USA would have interested Igino and that no doubt was the subject of their conversation. Prezzolini was already a distinguished writer (he continued so almost up to the time of his death at the age of 90 in 1982) and always in the centre of controversy. When he was later accused by an American professor of using *Casa Italiana* of Columbia University as a centre of propaganda for Fascism, he convincingly cleared himself, referring back to his long association with Columbia University in New York, as early as 1923. For many years, he kept close contact with the Italian immigrants in the USA. He spent a good part of his life in the USA. He was always controversial.

The Vatican Library

Igino Giordani began working at the Vatican Library in August 1928. He at once applied himself to introduce the most modern method of cataloguing to the most ancient – indeed Byzantine library. Until his method was used, it

*ibid. p.80.

took a day's work to find a book. After many years of work, using all the knowledge he had acquired in America and methods he had observed at the Washington Library of Congress, it was possible to find almost any book in half an hour. Not that this efficiency pleased everybody. Some had enjoyed the hunt and for them the social event had been more important than actually reading the book they had found. Skills were acquired and some had developed their own method of discovering books which they confidentially passed on to others. New boys would be dazzled by the way old hands found their books.

Fifty years later when I made an historic visit to the famous library with Giordani we stood awhile in the beautiful Belvedere Court and it was full of cars. 'My cataloguing', he said, 'has brought all these people here and ruined the view – it is *bel*-vedere no longer'. But it was a remarkable achievement which the librarian Harnack, son of the famous Berlin theologian, described as fifty years ahead of all the libraries of Europe. He worked steadily in those years, from 7am until 1pm and then to his books, reading, summarizing and writing.

A visit to the past

On 19th September 1979, I had the great privilege of visiting the Vatican Library with Igino Giordani. He had not been there for about 25 years. We drove in from Rocca di Papa and it was a tiring drive for him in the Roman traffic. I was worried because Igino looked tired after a sleepless night. But as we drove into the Vatican City and then went to the Belvedere Courtyard, all tiredness went from his face. He felt the inspiration of his magnificent work half a century before. A statue of the second century Christian teacher, Hippolytus, greeted us as we entered. Pope John XXIII had removed it from San Giovanni in Laterana, cleaned it and placed it where it belonged at the entrance to the *Biblioteca Vaticana*. The tables for the date of Easter were clearly carved on the side of his episcopal chair and they were clearly wrong! We waited and I was not sorry to have the time to examine the many treasures in the entrance hall. But Igino had been promised immediate entry into his former kingdom. Telephone confirmation was needed and it seemed to take longer than necessary. The real delay was to find someone senior enough to greet him. He did not chafe, but with characteristic humour said: 'We have the oldest bureaucracy in the world. Given to us by the Roman Emperors!' We took the lift up to the first floor where Giordani had worked for so many years. His mind was back there and in his attractive English he threw out information: 'My desk was at the end there; here is where De Gasperi sat. In this room we had the first Council Meetings of the D.C. (*Democrazia Cristiana*)'. It was clear from his words that these were not organized meetings but deep discussions of ideas and a historical analysis that would later form the basis of political action.

The present director treated Giordani like his master: 'I was one of his pupils', he said with pride, 'but who will follow me?' We lingered long enough in that busy cataloguing room to catch the atmosphere of years ago. Giordani checked to see whether they were keeping his system up to date!

Apart from giving to the oldest library the most modern cataloguing system, he also founded a library school were young librarians, including the present director, were trained. This director was still with us and he took us to the new School of Library Science. They can now take 80 students at a time – and about 120 apply. A plaque in the crowded classroom tells of its restoration in 1941 under Pope Pius XII, who as Cardinal Pacelli had appointed Igino Giordani director of the school in 1936. It was the same room as Giordani had known and used, where he had taught future librarians who later spread all over Europe, taking Giordani's system with them. It was more crowded now and somewhat changed to accommo-date many more students.

We went to the second floor to the Records and Igino explained the cataloguing system to me. He was still master of his craft in his 80s, and he was much moved as he remembered. As I looked through the cards, I was surprised to find how little was there from the pen of Dietrich Bonhoeffer. His father's book on 'Psychology' was there, but only one Dutch book dealt with this most seminal of theologians. I felt that had Giordani been there, the books of Dietrich Bonhoeffer would have been well represented. Even in the thirties he was aware of ecumenical theology and classifying it. We proceeded to the Reading Room, which is beautiful. The Vatican is full of the most breath-taking rooms. After looking at the shelves of *Stampati*, ie. printed books and journals, all neatly bound and easily accessible, we passed to the manuscripts. The age of the library is evident when you realize the number of books that are in manuscript because they were before the age of printing. These too are catalogued with the most modern system.

We remained in this lovely library as long as Giordani could stand the strain. It had been a momentous morning for him and he talked of the days in Fascist Italy when he carried on his own war against Mussolini from these beautiful halls. We stepped out into the sunshine in the

Belvedere Courtyard and regretted the cars. He was tired, physically and emotionally. At every turn he had been received like a patriarch. The niece of Pope Pius XII, whose biography he had written and who owed a great deal to Giordani, greeted him warmly.

7

The Cradle of the Christian Democrats

Alcide De Gasperi, whom Igino Giordani describes in his biography as the 'saviour of Italy', was threatened in the early days of Fascism. We have seen now Giordani defended him in print. The time soon came, when Giordani was safely established in the Vatican Library, for a much more physical protection. In 1929, De Gasperi came out of prison and sent a card to Giordani – the postcard of a lonely man – saying that he did not see many friends these days and that he usually had his lunch at a *trattoria* near the Pantheon (Rotunda).★

Giordani responded at once. He met him and discovered how much he was in need of protection. With other colleagues, he applied for De Gasperi to be appointed to the cataloguing staff of the Vatican Library. The application was made to Monsignor Giovanni Mercati who asked no questions. De Gasperi was appointed to fill in cards and help with the heavy task of cataloguing. De Gasperi had no qualifications for the job; but everybody knew that he was not there for that. He was there for his own protection and for the more important task of preparing a government for Italy when Fascism fell.

★ *'Memorie'*, p.90.

In April 1929, De Gasperi joined Igino Giordani, Carmelo Scalia, Monsignor Benedetti, Gerardo Bruni, etc. All were described as librarians. Every day between periods of work, they would meet to discuss the future government of Italy. In his biography of Alcide de Gasperi, Giordani writes of those meetings:

that stern atmosphere of study and thought remained under Fascism, like a rock of resistance, a ferment of freedom. The card-cataloguing department seemed at the time to be like a miniature parliament. The study habits and critical methods helped to confer a tone of objectivity on the daily political surveys and in the light of that objectivity, Fascism revealed its true nature, both as the moral decadence of man and the precarious political system it was.

We were certain, and De Gasperi asserted it with more authority than anyone else, that Mussolini would have dragged Italy into war and into ruin. Just as Sturzo had always said.*

Police surveillance

The meetings were clandestine, but it was perfectly obvious to the Political Police Department that this kind of consultation was going on. If they had had the power, there is no doubt that they would have raided the Vatican Library. But for the time being, the conspirators were safe. Giordani wrote: 'One day, Count De Vecchi of Val Cismon, a member of the quadumvirate and Italy's ambassador to the Holy See, expressed cautious criticism of the Holy Father's government because he offered work and refuge to several anti-Fascists, especially De Gasperi. The Pope courteously but firmly answered him:

* 'Alcide De Gasperi', Montadori, Milan, 1955, p.110.

'We are delighted to have been able to give bread to De Gasperi who was without work'. Giordani added to this: 'A year and a half of prison, a stay in hospital, and a wait for work had used up the scarce resources of his family, so that Alcide, even after his service in the Vatican, had to work extremely hard to pay his debts and cope with his domestic difficulties'.*

Documents made available after the war show that information about the 'well-known Giordani' and the 'ex-parliamentary member for the Popular Party, Alcide De Gasperi' were occasionally the subject of Police despatches. One such despatch dated 15th October XVIII (i.e. 1940) reads:

> Reliable and confidential sources have it that the well-known Giordani, Igino – previously referred to in note 500.13151, 21st May last – has kept close contact with ex-parliamentary member for the Popular Party Alcide De Gasperi . . . Even though both Giordani and De Gasperi have tried to keep their relations secret . . . from that time *from when they were able to act freely* dates their common understanding and political activity that was and remains without doubt contrary to Fascism.†

In his biography of *Alcide De Gasperi*, Giordani describes how after Mussolini had taken Italy into the war, these activities intenstified. De Gasperi clearly took the lead, discussing future party policy with Christian Democrats whom he was able to meet in the Library. He discussed future governments also with anti-fascists of other parties. And in all these meetings, Igino Giordani was present and playing his part politically. The Political Police Department had every reason to be worried about these meetings. They were the centre of resistance to the regime.

* ibid. p.110f..
† *'Memorie'*, p.91f..

The early writings of Giordani

While it was soon evident that De Gasperi was a politician and could never be anything else, Gordani threw himself into the immediate task of librarianship and developed his skills as a writer.

This period in the Vatican Library represents the first of two long periods rich in publication. As writer, journalist, editor, he had shown skills already. In particular, his political articles had been admired, feared and envied. He had supplemented his income in America with articles readily accepted. And we need to remember that this was the period of the Depression with strong competition for any work that could earn extra money. You had to be good to meet that kind of competition.

We have already seen how Piero Gobetti, one of the most involved anti-Fascist writers in Turin, had recognized the quality of Igino Giordani's writing and asked him to compile 'Rivolta Cattolica'. Although Gobetti was much younger than Giordani, he had already made his mark. He had been closely associated with the Communists and Antonio Gramsci, and since 1922 was the editor of the weekly, 'Rivoluzione liberale'. Gobetti was well known and a marked man. From 1924, the year in which he had asked Igino to edit his articles for 'Rivolta Cattolica', the Fascists were determined to get him. Repeated beatings made life impossible for him in Turin and he had to flee to Paris, where he died in 1926 as a result of the beatings he received at the hands of the Fascists. No doubt when Igino met Prezzolini in Paris, so soon after the tragic death of their mutual friend, he was stirred by what he heard of Gobetti's last days from one who was there at the end.

In the Vatican Library Giordani had easy and daily access to the best library he had ever known. A new writer emerged in these conditions. He was not hiding in the Vatican Library, he was discovering its riches. His early love of the Fathers of the Church was stimulated and fed. He read widely and soon equipped himself to become a leading apologist for the Catholic Faith. He had the pen of a Tertullian, to ridicule foolish error and to defend the authenticity of the Faith. He never quite lost the style of Tertullian. Both writers had a way with unbelievers and heretics!

By 1930, he had six important books to his credit:

1. *Sister Crocifissa Militerni,*★ a small book in size, only 63 pages, but profound in its analysis and description. It is one of the fruits of his American visit. Sister Crocifissa was the mother superior of the Sisters of St. John the Baptist, whom he had met in Long Island. The order impressed him and it represented one more step forward in his life-long search for St. Catherine of Siena, who increasingly became his guiding light.

2. *Saint John Chrysostom,*† a rather larger book, published in Padua in 1929 which shows how well he had used his opportunities in the Vatican Library to master the writings of this prince of preachers.

3. *Saint Justin Martyr,*‡ a book to which he gave the subtitle, 'Apologetics.' This work, published in Florence in the same year, took him back to the earlier writings of the Fathers, contemporary with Tertullian. He was seeking here a way of reconciling the Faith with responsibility for a secular world. He could not have written this without his experiences in America but there are signs that his political involvement in Italy helped him to understand Justin Martyr better. His various worlds

★ *'Suor Crocifissa Militerni, delle suore di San Giovanni Battista',* Rome, 1926.
† *'San Giovanni Crisostomo',* Libreria Gregoriana, Padua, 1929.
‡ *'San Giustino Martire',* Fiorentina, Florence, 1929.

were coming together. There was only one Giordani and whether he was defending De Gasperi or explaining St. Chrysostom, there was an integrity about the man.

4. *Quaternary America,** an extravagant novel which helped him to put down on paper all the contradictory things he was thinking about America. The title is taken from geology – quaternary period being the one after the tertiary. His criticism and his kindly love of America combine.

5. *Montalembert.†* An early hero of Giordani, a liberal Catholic like himself who combined a profound faith with deep political concern. He was also the founder of a newspaper, 'L'Avvenire'. This is really two books. In 1925, he published a biography of this French Catholic political writer and then in 1930, an anthology of his writings.‡ Both by the same publishing firm in Turin.

The second of these Montalembert books was published under a pseudonym, Adolfo Tommasi. He used this pseudonym frequently in articles he wrote for 'Fides'.

6. *The First Christian Polemic.*§ This was a study of the Apologists of the 2nd century – Irenaeus, Tertullian, Justin Martyr, etc. Again it showed his growing concern with a period in the history of the Church with which he felt closely identified. It was a period which always dominated his interest. The book, published in Brescia, went through several editions and eventually carried the subtitle 'The Greek Apologists of the Second Century'.

There was also another book, which he had started in America, a collection of modern American writers, translated into Italian.

* *'L'America quaternaria'*, Soc. Apostolato Stampa, Rome, 1930.
† *'Montalembert (Dio e libertà)'*, SEI, Turin, 1925.
‡ *'Montalembert (Antologia)'*, SEI, Turin, 1930.
§ *'La prima polemica cristiana'*, Morcelliana, Brescia, 1927.

106

'Fides'

Meanwhile, in all this activity of studying and writing, he carried on the editorship of 'Fides', which was not just a Catholic review, it was *the* Catholic review. By means of it, he helped to form the minds of priests throughout Italy and bring to them the teaching of the world Church in historical depth. He was required to edit this review, which was the monthly organ of the Pontifical Commission for the Preservation of the Faith. He had a difficult time at first, because he was constantly trying to broaden its views. The Pontifical Commission saw it as a journal to 'maintain' the Faith, not to widen the horizon! Giordani had been far more influenced by America than he realized at the time. It was not only library science that he learnt there. And his lively contacts, which wherever he went he found irresistible, brought him copies of journals to add to the many that came from other parts of the world. The result was that at times the monthly 'Fides' was like a window on the world for an isolated Italy. And it was not only the Catholics who interested him. He could attack heresey as fiercely as any Catholic writer, but he could not disguise from himself the fact that there were men and women of faith, a faith like his own outside the Catholic Church. His interest in the ecumenical movement, which came largely from Anglo-Saxon sources, grew. He wrote a great deal about Protestantism, although he often condemned it. There are many articles in 'Fides' which give the Church of England a rough time. There are even fiercer articles condemning the dollar evangelism of American missions. Yet despite his ready condemnation of what he believed to be a dangerous divergence from the true Church, he saw in Protestantism more than heresy and schism. He recognized the hand of God in bringing the separated Churches together. No doubt he saw this as the beginning of a movement that would eventually lead them all back to Rome. He was a staunch supporter of the truth of the Church and committed to the authority of the Church of Rome, although he would always call it the Catholic Church and insist that that meant universal. He compromised no more in Church matters than he did in political. Yet, there were exciting things happening as the young ecumenical movement grew that led him to follow it closely.

The First World Conference on Faith and Order took place in Lausanne in 1927. It was Protestant and Anglican; but it received more sympathetic treatment in 'Fides' than in many Protestant periodicals, where it was largely ignored.

Political issues in 'Fides'

It was inevitable that Giordani should occasionally overstep the limits placed upon his mandate by the Pontifical Commission and it was equally inevitable that he should get himself involved in political issues. Giordani saw his task as defending the Church and also educating it in the political issues of the day. An example can be seen in the way in which Catholic Action was handled. Pope Pius XI in his various concordats throughout Europe defended the rights of Catholic Action. This was to become a highly controversial issue with the German States later and it was not without difficulty even in Spain. But in Italy, it was essential that Catholic Action should be allowed to operate freely so long as it was not subversive of the state. A battle raged between Pope Pius XI and Mussolini on this very issue. This came to a head in July 1931 and Giordani covered the contoversy in great detail in 'Fides'. He showed a clear grasp of the issues and was courageous in his statement of them. These articles in 'Fides' were more than the echo of the Papal Commission, they were the work of an original mind. Giordani recognized that he was not dealing with old issues, but that he was dealing with new situations such as had not existed in Europe since the days of the Roman Empire and the martyrs. And apart from the articles in 'Fides' and elsewhere, it led him into a whole new writing programme.

A sign of contradiction

The controversy over Catholic Action gave rise to what Giordani describes as his first important book *'Segno di Contraddizione'* (Sign of Contradiction).* It dealt with the issues of Church and State.'. . . the most tremendous religious, and therefore social dilemma', he wrote, '[is] . . . whether there is a Church and a State, or simply a Church-State, which is atheism married to idolatry'.†

When Daniel-Rops translated that book, he called it *'La Revolution de la Croix'* ('The Revolution of the Cross'). In an introduction to the French translation, Daniel-Rops gave us a glimpse of Giordani's life during this period which shows the emergence of a new theological assessment of political power. The French introduction was thought important enough many years later to be translated into Italian for the fifth edition of *'Segno di Contraddizione'* in 1954. As glimpses of his life are rare enough in the twenties, I shall quote at length from the French 'Introduction':

* *'Segno di contraddizione'*, Morcelliana, Brescia, 1933.
† op. cit., p.11.

In Rome, in a little house, whose garden overlooked part of the City (in fact from the balcony you could see the ruined walls of the Colosseum), four of us met together as friends. Our host (Don Giuseppe De Luca) spoke of Communism and Christianity; he was a young priest with his heart on fire: 'Are you not afraid,' he said, 'when you think that some of the highest Christian values can be discovered among those fighting against Christianity? You can discover them subverted, betrayed in their intentions, unrecognizable . . . and yet . . . Is not the worker who sacrifices himself for an Ideal worth more than a bourgeois egoist who limits himself to going to elegant masses!' Then one of those present who had listened in silence throughout the whole conversation so far, said in a quiet voice: 'Perhaps we are near to the time when Christ must be among us as a sign of contradiction'. Then he soberly outlined the times that we were approaching in which there could be no flight nor cowardice, but times of dilemma, when it would be necessary to stand alone between the kingdom of God and the kingdom of the Beast.*

The quiet speaker was Igino Giordani, and Daniel-Rops goes on to say that when he read the books of Giordani again, he realized what a unique place he held among the young Catholic writers of Italy. He placed him with French Catholic writers like Léon Bloy and Charles Péguy. At that time, these two writers, both of whom had died during the First World War, were exercising an enormous influence on the Catholic renewal which was sweeping across France. Daniel-Rops saw Giordani as more than a 'polemicist' for Catholicism, he saw him as an 'apologist'. He fought and he denounced, but above all he affirmed. He was not concerned with the details of polemics, but with the much larger issues of the 'apostolate'.

Like all who read Giordani's writings in this period,

* ibid. p.7.

Daniel-Rops was deeply impressed by the patristic scholarship, which showed not only the knowledge he had acquired from his youth, but also the strong influence of certain Fathers of the Church upon his political thinking:

> Igino Giordani examines Christianity as a true revolution, produced historically in a given time and a given place, but which is eternally being renewed in the midst of us.*

This early important book by Giordani deals with the nature of the Christian revolution. It is a 'bloody' revolution in a world drunk with blood, but it is the blood of Christ and of his saints that is spilt, not of the enemy. The role of the Christian is to testify to the cross, to suffer and to witness unto death. He draws upon the early Fathers and the time of the martyrs, justifying this by a comparison between the age in which he lived and that of the second and third century. This is no superficial comparison. He had studied both periods with care. His own day was a time when dictators were arising demanding absolute obedience. In any country, a Mussolini, a Hitler, a Chang-Kai-Shek, a Franco could arise. It had nothing to do with national characteristics. Given the right economic and social conditions, pagan dictators could have arisen in Britain, France, America, Russia. He was very shrewd in his assessment of the signs of the times. Equally, he knew his second and third century. Certainly he said, paganism has changed its name: 'it is now called eugenics or racism, materialism or laicism, it takes up residence in "Quaternary America", lodges on the edges of the Mediterranean and for idols, the Babbitts and the rockets instead of statues of marble. But whatever its form, it is the old human error of worshipping the creature rather than the Creator.'

* ibid. p.8.

After *'Segno di Contraddizione'* he developed the same theme in later years in *'Il messaggio sociale di Gesù'* (The Social Message of Jesus)* which was translated into English and published in separate sections as 'The Social Teaching of the Gospels', and 'The Social Teaching of the early Church Fathers'. The whole was written first in 1935 and translated much later (1943–1944).

'Semi di Sangue' (The Seed of the Martyrs)† appeared in the same year; and a few years later a novel of the time of Hildebrandt, *'La Città Murata'* (The Walled City),‡ which was Tivoli.

'Frontespizio'

Despite this considerable output in books, Giordani was writing even more in articles for weeklies and reviews. His main output was in 'Fides', where much of the material we discussed in the last section first appeared. He wrote under many pseudonyms and his own name. I detected a comparison, perhaps conscious imitation, of Kierkegaard. But I was never able to prove that his pseudonyms had any separate life of their own (as in Kierkegaard). Giordani is all too easily recognized in them all! He was a man of integrity even in his pseudonyms. No one was fooled. But there were certain restrictions on 'Fides', while he needed also a political outlet and this he obtained when he agreed to write a regular page for 'Frontespizio'.

The editor, Piero Bargellini, approached Giordani to

---

* *'Il messaggio sociale di Gesù'*, in four volumes: 1. *Gli Evangelisti;* 2. *Gli Apostoli;* 3. *I Primi Padri della Chiesa*; 4. *I Grandi Padri della Chiesa,* SEI, Turin, 1935.

† Morcelliana, Brescia, 1935.

‡ L'Illustrazione Vaticana, Rome, 1936

write 'Page Seven' of 'Frontespizio'. The letter was dated 30th July 1930. It pointed out the danger of this influential weekly being closed. It was edited quite brilliantly by Bargellini and published in Florence. It was in danger of closing for lack of subscribers. In the letter he pointed out that only three things could save the paper: the help of God, the collaboration of good writers and a financial subsidy. Giordani could hardly resist an appeal like that. He was persuaded and regularly wrote 'Page Seven'. He was soon at odds with other writers, particularly with Papini. As long as it lasted, 'Frontespizio' was the main outlet for his political writings. 'Fides' remained his paper and despite the difficulties he had in satisfying the Establishment, he was respected and sometimes feared as a leading Catholic apologist throughout the Fascist period.

The long shelf of bound volumes of 'Fides' which ran the length of his flat in Rocca di Papa contained a record of his life and thought during that period. The editoral address given in the review was Via Gioberti, 60. This is the side entrance to a large building near S. Maria Maggiore, on the corner of Via Napoleone III and Via Gioberti, whose insignia show still that it once belonged to the Church, although part of it, the part which Giordani used, appears now to be used by the Italian State. The earlier address must have pleased him more, it was *Via dell' Umiltà*.

Differences with De Gasperi

Igino Giordani and Alcide De Gasperi made a complementary pair. Giordani was the scholar, writer, journalist, a lay tertiary of the Dominican Order, passionately attached to his Church and its teaching, an apologist for

113

the Church, a Christian with a backbone. De Gasperi was a politician with the makings already of a statesman; a political figure with shrewd judgement, a knowledge of people, a master of the 'art of the possible', a lay Catholic who had aspirations to spirituality, but whose vocation was to political leadership. They needed each other at this crucial stage and the Christian Democratic Party in process of formation needed them both. Giordani gave the Party its basic principles and De Gasperi gave it its policy. It was inevitable that policy and principle should diverge at times. So far, that divergence was minor, later it would become much more serious.

In 1944, the difference showed itself over a newspaper. Giordani had been given the task of preparing and founding a Catholic newspaper to be called 'Il Quotidiano'. De Gasperi thought this was a mistake. The new paper would inevitably compete with 'Il Popolo', the organ of the Christian Democratic Party (DC). 'Il Quotidiano' was published and Giordani was its director until 1946. He remained true to what he had written in *'Segno di Contraddizione'*.

From 1946 to 1953 De Gasperi and Giordani were again active in the political life of the Country, but with different tasks and positions. De Gasperi was to lead the Christian Democrats to power; Giordani worked for the Party quietly and conscientiously, but in the background. Two comments bring out the difference at this stage very clearly. Of De Gasperi, Giordani writes:

> He was a man of action, a shrewd observer of the times, ready to adapt and expand his ideology systematically and pragmatically. He did not always keep to the rules of the Party, nor confine himself to its limits. Italy had to be reconstructed and there was more need for action than words.★

★ 'Alcide De Gasperi', op. cit..

114

Of Giordani, Passo Perduto writes in 'La Via' in 1952:

> He was a writer and a scholar, a man opposed to Communists without qualification, both at the intellectual and the moral level. He felt it necessary to speak the truth at all times. He maintained very definite, almost rigid moral values in politics and religion. Within the Party he was considered an idealist and somewhat 'ingenious'.

As De Gasperi developed the *Democrazia Cristiana* to become the ruling Party in Italy, there was an inevitable amount of compromise, existing side by side with a ruthless insistence upon conformity. This is the way of all successful parties and the DC was successful under De Gasperi. Until quite recently, despite necessary conditions, the leaders of the DC assumed that they are those who 'have the right to rule'. But within such a Party, an idealist is uneasy. Giordani became rather like the 'leader of the internal opposition'. He could not keep quiet and insisted upon criticizing the Party when all it wanted was support. The Party needed his pen to devastate other parties, but he sometimes turned it upon his own! Giordani was valuable when he was defending the Party, which he often did; but he was embarrassing when he challenged the Party to new ideas, when the same acid pen which won so many victories for the DC criticized it all too effectively. Much of the criticism came out in 'La Via', a weekly which Giordani also edited.

At the conclusion of the Annual Party Conference, 18-20th December 1949, De Gasperi publicly denounced several publications as disapproved of, by the Party, a kind of political index, and he included among them 'La Via'.

Giordani responded at once:

> If a sincere criticism cannot be tolerated . . . the freedom of democracy is finished. We are sure that we are serving the DC better with our criticism than we would with our

silence, or worse still our flattery. We have too much esteem for the democratic principles of the Hon. Alcide de Gasperi, and we have demonstrated too much friendship in the years of trial, to do him the wrong of hiding from him what the nation feels. The DC is both Democratic and Christian and therefore we feel that it cannot behave like other, totalitarian parties which insist upon a conformity of mind at the price of suppressing the truth.*

But this has taken us well beyond the days when the Christian Democrats were cradled in the Vatican Library, and even beyond that crucial meeting with Chiara Lubich which was eventually to change the whole direction of Giordani's life.

* 'La Via', January 1950

8

The Second World War and After

There was no chance of Giordani being called up for his second war! The First World War had left him for dead and he survived only by his indomitable will. He survived, but as a war casualty, crippled and unfit for war service. He had hardly entered the First World War, where so many young Italians volunteered with zeal, with patriotic fervour or enthusiasm. He went because he had to. But once in uniform, he was brave enough and saw some point in liberating Italian lands from alien domination. He fought a good war and was wounded gallantly.

But this second war was different. There were few volunteers this time. For Giordani, the second war made no sense at all. It was simply a desired opportunity for dictators to exercise themselves and seek glory. As Giordani was so radically opposed to Mussolini and consequently to Hitler, although he said nothing about Franco, the war was an unmitigated folly and Italy's entry into it, sheer disaster. He was not carried away by the exuberant boasts of the Fascists that the dictators would sweep away the effete Democracies because they had old-fashioned weapons while the states of Germany and Italy had the latest equipment. The new nations, the new empires were like musical comedies and he knew that they could not carry through their boasts. With America, Britain, France and most of the world, against them, the Dictatorship could win only quick and early victories. At first, the success of Hitler's *Blitzkrieg* in France seemed to confirm their boasts, but it was only a matter of time. Despite its obvious stupidity, Italy joined the war on the side of the Germans, a little late, but with great enthusiasm for the prizes to be won.

Anti-semitism

The alliance with Germany increased the anti-semitism, which Giordani did not share: 'In imitation or obedience to the Führer, anti-semitism grew in Italy', he writes.* One of his relatives by marriage took refuge in America and there was some talk of the parents hiding with the Giordanis. The Italians did not accept this persecution of the Jews in the way the Germans did. They hid their Jews. A contemporary of Giordani's who talked with me one night in Rome, said with a proud and sure boast: 'We Italians may sometimes have been cowards, but we protected our Jews!' And the Giordanis were prepared also to do this. It happened that the husband found security while his wife went back to collect some belongings and was arrested. She was taken off, Giordani writes with anger, 'in wagons of human flesh to the concentration camps'.† This part-Jewish family appears to be the only one with whom he was associated, although he was accused of hiding Jews in the Vatican Library. Giordani was not anti-semitic, but he did not feel called to take any strenuous action on behalf of the

* '*Memorie*', p.99.
† ibid. p.99f..

Jews. His vocation lay elsewhere. This did not prevent Roberto Farrinacci from attacking the Holy See in his Cremona newspaper with the words that involved Giordani: 'perhaps under the influence of the director, Igino Giordani, the Holy See is sheltering not a few Jews in the *Scuola di Biblioteconomia'*.*

Personal grief

It was during these war years that his parents died. His mother died in 'silence, as she had lived'. In his autobiography, Igino Giordani paused at this point to pay a tender tribute to his mother:

> I found myself thinking of her as a nun, from the moment when all her actions were done, day and night, with God in mind, in union with God, immersed in that true humility which is an atmosphere of being totally available to God.†

She never knew how to read or write, her interior devotion was built up from sermons and meditations which she had heard, stimulated by pictures and colours. She laboured without ceasing.

> When she seemed ill [Giordani wrote] we children insisted upon taking her to a clinic so that she would have a chance of recovery. At the clinic in Rome she had the necessary surgery. During the operation, her soul ever united to God, simply passed over at the critical hour.‡

He loved her but without much expression of that love; it was to his father that he seemed most attached. But in 1941, he wrote about her in his diary as though all the years he had kept back an emotion. What Igino

* ibid. p.100.
† ibid..
‡ ibid..

Giordani says then about his mother illuminates the man.

I cannot think of my mother without rising again to the thought of Christ's mother, because her destiny as a working-class woman, one who lived in suffering and want, in unremitting toil, recalls to me the image of that Israelite maiden, pierced by seven swords. She was still alive – before she died amidst the torments of a surgical operation better described as a butchery – and already the thought of her and the image of her brought me more anguish than tenderness, because that stern face, the face of an Etruscan woman, bore marks and reminders of suffering, her own and that of her kinsfolk, that of a whole tragic generation. Her smile issued from the threshold of a spasm of pain, she smiled for us, but she was suffering, mourning and praying within herself. Not given to displays of feeling, she rarely kissed her children, except when they were going away or when they were returning from long absences; but in her reserve, she lived for them and wore herself out for them; she devoured them with her eyes; she waited up for them at night, saying rosaries, and then, at their return, she made it her business to fortify their spirit, in order to sow in it, all unlettered as she was, the seeds of the knowledge of God. She was drained of blood when she died: and it was an offering to Christ, from whom she had drawn all her sustenance. *

The honest prayers of a labouring man

In November 1942, Giordani's father died. The passage describing that night in his autobiography has much the same brave sense of sorrow and admiration which marks the passage describing the death of his mother. This man had led him in the ways of truth, he had taken him to

* 'Diary of fire', New City, London, 1981, p.7f..

120

Mass, introduced him to the confraternity, told him of the Jesuits, understood his early admiration and awe before Father Mancini, taught him to lay bricks and build honestly. If in later years he had grown away from his father, he had never lost his admiration for a man who could hold his head up anywhere. All this is remembered in the moment of his death:

> As soon as I received notice of the crisis, I rushed to Tivoli and arrived at the hospital in total darkness, where with great difficulty I at last succeeded in getting some news. The news was that father was dead and that his body lay in the mortuary.*

These were the conditions of war time black-outs, with Rome in danger of becoming a battlefield. Mercifully, it was not fought over or reduced to rubble like Berlin and Cologne, but it was subject to bombing. He found his father in the mortuary and then the son meditated upon the hard life of his labouring father:

> Incessant labour had brought him to this place, where by the light of a candle, I looked again at that honest face which was born to suffering at the hands of others. Early that morning he had been up to attend the celebrations in the Church, dressed as a brother of the confraternity. He was participating when he died, fallen before the altar like a sacrifice.†

What memories of his boyhood held him in that darkened place.

A child of the poor

These two descriptions of the death of mother and father tell us a great deal about Igino Giordani. This was his

* 'Memorie', p.101.
† ibid..

stock and there he learnt to admire the humility of the poor. He was born in poverty and he never failed to serve the poor. He knew that poverty could be grinding and degrading, but he also knew that only in the face of the poor could you see the face of Christ. His whole life, he despised pride and loved humility. This deep rooted realism about the poor and sense of spiritual depth in poverty enabled this son of proletarian parents to look anyone in the face without subservience. He could instruct a Pope without arrogance; he would not toady for a place on De Gasperi's Cabinet. As he watched his mother die and looked upon the face of his dead father, he recognized and acknowledged true Christian dignity. The sufferings of the poor were for him a key to under-standing the sufferings of Christ. He knew that his first and deepest impressions of Christ and the Virgin were gained from such a father and such a mother.

The war threatens Rome

For the first two years, the war was far from Rome and caused little disturbance to the Giordani family life. Igino and his wife Mya were too intelligent not to know that eventually this war would have far reaching consequences for them all. But for a while, the radio announced historic and fantastic victories. Life went on in Rome much as before, although black-out conditions by the end of 1942 and shortage of food and ordinary things affected the poor. Once the battle for Italy had started it was always possible that Rome might become a battle-field. The surrender to the American and British troops at Salerno and the armistice on 8th September 1943 did not take Italy out of the war, but simply made her into a country occupied by both sides. Rome was in the hands of the Germans. But there was no great disturbance in the Giordani family.

The family

It was 20 years since the Giordani wedding in Tivoli, 2nd February 1920. The first home had been modest rooms in Via Cavour with the Waldensian family. Mya was a singer and for many years, her singing filled the home with Spring. She created a bastion for Igino against the violence and hatred outside, she kept him human as he became a famous writer and political guide.

They had four children. The first, Mario, was born in 1926, with Igino in hospital with a high fever, and soon he had to leave to go to America. Mario was a doctor from his youth, who became a distinguished surgeon. There were two more boys: Sergio, born in 1929, who became a film producer and travelled the world, once much later with his father into Asia; Ildebrando, named when Igino was working on his novel, 'The Walled City', which was about Tivoli in the time of Hildenbrandt (Ildebrando in Italian). Ildebrando also followed the visual arts and has a responsible job today in TV. For many years there were only these three boys. Eventually a girl was born: Bonizza in 1937. As Igino tells us in his book about the family, *'La Repubblica dei Marmocchi'** ('The Toddlers' Republic'), the boys were not at all sure about the admission of a girl to their republic. She was eventually accepted into this happy family. Thus in 1943, this was a family with three boys aged 17, 14 and 12 and with a little girl of 6. Later editions of 'The Toddlers' Republic' were illustrated by Bonizza, who showed

* *'La repubblica dei marmocchi'*, Citta Nuovà, Rome, (IVth edition,) pp. 15-18.

distinct artistic ability and who later developed skills in book illustration, dress design and decor for TV sets.

'The family', writes Giordani in this attractive book, 'is an autocracy which rapidly becomes a republic, a children's republic'. The picture of family life in this book shows Giordani as a delightful and slightly harassed father, working hard, often distracted by the children but loving them all dearly. Early in the book, he points out that you cannot write about education or children if you have children around. The practice makes every theory untenable.

The war comes to Rome

This family life was untroubled by war until 1943. Carolina Marchi in her book on the *'Palazzo Margherita'*, sketches this phoney wartime of Rome in a few words:

> Via Veneto continued to be a glamorous meeting place. The cafés were crowded and stopping at Rosati's for a noontime aperitif was still considered very chic. *

But all this changed as the war came closer:

> Rome too was bombarded. The change continued after the armistice of September 1943, when the Germans occupied Rome. Senior German officers were quartered in the big hotels, Kesselring stayed at the 'Flora'; and the Commandant of the City of Rome, General Maeltzer, a gourmet and wine lover, took up residence at the 'Excelsior'. . . He organized lavish dinners and parties, while armed guards patrolled the streets.
>
> During the first five months of 1944, Via Veneto and most of the Ludovisi quarter (the elegant quarter of Rome, from the days of the ancient Republican families) were barricaded from the rest of the city. The Romans had to give up their evening strolls. The German curfew

* Carolina Marchi, op. cit., p.45.

varied day by day . . . and the Romans had to go back early to the empty larders of their cold black lodgings. And even by day, such world famous Roman streets as Via Condotti, Piazza di Spagna, and Via del Corso, not to mention Via Veneto, remained deserted; stores had nothing to sell, and customers nothing to spend.*

Evacuees

The Giordanis were not given to glamorous nights in the Via Veneto, nor to drinking their noontime aperitif at Rosati's. That was not their world, But, in his autobiography, Giordani also describes the changed conditions, as they affected the family:

In the summer of 1943, I sent the family to Capranica Prenestina (about as far from Rome as Tivoli and in a country area), I visited them because I wanted to hide some American soldiers who had slipped through the Monte Cassino line. One day (I was not there on this occasion, but in Rome), some German soldiers were prowling around the district insulting and disarming the Italian Carabinieri and soldiers of the guard. My son, Mario, who saw them was angered by this humiliation and he shouted at the Germans in an aggressive tone, 'Addosso ai nazisti!' [An equivalent translation of that abusive phrase might be, 'Throttle the Nazis!]

Luckily the Germans did not understand, or perhaps if they did, a mere boy was no threat to them. They left him alone and very quickly his mother rescued him, while the German soldiers went on to another town.†

Giordani describes a little of the conditions he met on another visit and the scene in Rome when the Germans arrived:

I arrived from Rome, taking the tram into the country as

* ibid..
† 'Memorie', p. 103

125

far as Palestrina, and then climbed up the hill on foot for about two hours, made the more painful by my leg which was still hurting . . . Then came September. I was in Rome. The Nazis entered, the government fled with the King to Brindisi. Offices closed, streets deserted, no food, no traffic.*

He tells us that he was able to shelter and came to no harm. There were many in Rome, ready and willing to give shelter to the *'anti-fascisti'* and that certainly descri-bed Giordani. He returned to Capranica as soon as he could, but he tired of the country. The black market was at its height and anyone from Rome was fair game in the country. He gives examples of exorbitant prices charged. It was also no safer in the countryside around Rome, which was as much exposed to raids as Rome itself. Giordani's autobiography has a vivid description of travel in Italy as they returned to the *Città*. There were road blocks and inspections of baggage. The letters that Giordani had in his baggage could have caused much trouble, because they were from distinguished people throughout the world – none of them friendly to the Nazis. His baggage on inspection would have given enough evidence to convict him. But he had taken the precaution of acquiring a good supply of cigarettes, a gift from his friend the Chinese ambassador. With these, he came safely through the road blocks without inspection. I have no doubt that he was harmless like a dove, but he had the wisdom of serpents also at times.

The Germans leave Rome

The American and British troops, aided by great acts of heroism by Italian forces and guerrillas, moved steadily

* ibid. p. 102.

north and the Germans withdrew. There was a half agreement that Rome should be an Open City. That did not spare it the bombing, but it did mean that it was not fought over. Carolina Marchi catches the atmosphere of those days of liberation in a way that few have done:

The hotels on the Via Veneto began to empty in the last week of May 1944. Guards, patrols and barricades kept the population at bay during the German evacuation. One of the last Germans to leave on June 4th was General Maeltzer. All morning long, the Romans watched the German army pass by, on its way north. The drone of vehicles and the sound of marching troops filled the city. The exodus lasted all morning and into the afternoon. Then an ominous silence fell over the city. Even the distant cannon fire, which day by day had announced the approach of the Anglo-American forces, had stopped.

It was a splendid Sunday in June, one of those balmy sunny days that ease the soul and make Rome seem the most beautiful and hospitable city in the world. Almost all the Romans were indoors well before the six o'clock curfew, though many of them waited by their windows to watch the course of events.

Leaflets had been dropped from planes the night before with instructions from General Alexander: the population must maintain order and prevent sabotage. The Romans were more than cooperative. When they saw the first Allied vehicle arrive before sunset, they poured out into the streets *en masse* forgetting the curfew and the stern regulations that had governed their lives for so many months. Many of them spent the night on the street to watch columns of jeeps and tanks pass by, full of dust-covered soldiers with roses stuck in their camouflage helmets and Italian flags on their rifles. The moon was full that night, and the light on that extraordinary scene was almost as light as day.

Rome changed its aspect overnight. On the morning of Monday June 5, after a long Sunday of remarkable happenings, crowds of people from all over the city assembled at St. Peter's to pay their respects to Pope Pius XII, who had done so much to prevent the Holy City from being turned into a battlefield. Allied flags were flying all over Rome and streamers were hung with welcoming messages in English. The day before the walls had been covered with German propaganda posters alleging Allied atrocities. The city had undergone a stunning overnight transformation. *

Carolina Marchi continues her vivid description, but we have quoted enough. Giordani's own description of that day matches the sense of hope and feeling that, to quote Carolina Marchi again: 'The war was finally over, at least for Rome. Soon it would be over for the rest of Italy and for the world. Things would soon be fine'.

But for Giordani there was much to do. He had been meeting with De Gasperi, Cadorna, Bonomi and other leading anti-fascists in the modest parochial rooms of Monsignor Barbieri, Spataro and others. Their object was to prepare for the new political climate or at least for liberty.

As we have seen, the differences between De Gasperi and Giordani were growing and came to a head over the publication of 'Il Quotidiano', which was on the streets in time for the Liberation, however modest the issue. We must look more closely at that newspaper and the divergence between Giordani and De Gasperi.

'Il Quotidiano'

Alcide De Gasperi had a very clear objective. He sought the means whereby a Christian, Democratic, anti-Fascist Party could gain power and lead Italy out of the ruins created by Fascism and War. History tells of his success.

Giordani pondered long on the ideals of the *Partito*

---

* Carolina Marchi, op. cit., p.45ff.

*Igino Giordani, a young officer in the
Italian Army*

In hospital recovering from his wounds, 1918

CATHOLIC SCHOLARS IN THE UNITED STATES FOR IDEAS. Msgr. Enrico Benedetti, (second from left), Father Carmelo Scalia, (third from left), Prof. Gerardo Bruni, (left) and Prof. Ignio Giordani, members of the staff of the Vatican Library, have just come to this country to study the

Newspaper cutting just after Giordani had arrived in America, 1927

With some of his pupils in America

At the School of Library studies in the Vatican, Year I, 1934-35

Teaching in the seminary, 1942

*With his children Mario and
Bonizza in Rome, 1946*

Igino and his wife, Mya, in a family photograph during a festival in regional costume at the Villa d'Este, Tivoli, 1947: on the extreme right is Mya's brother

At Montecitorio, 1946

Don Luigi Sturzo

Giordani the politician, addressing a meeting of the Christian Democrats

Speaking at the twinning of Viterbo with Avignon, 1955: on the left is the Mayor of Viterbo, on the right the French Ambassador

As editor of the 'Quotidiano'

With Mya at Caux in Switzerland, 1948

With his colleagues in the library of the Italian Parliament

During his visit to Asia, 1959

At various Mariapolises: above left 1955, below left 1958, above and below right, the last Mariapolis in the Dolomites, 1959

*Giordani the ecumenist, presenting the Anglican Bishop
William Llewellyn to Pope Paul VI, 1967*

*At Rocca di Papa during the Second Vatican Council: from left to right, Fr Pasquale
Foresi, Igino Giordani, Canon Bernard Pawley, Mrs Margaret Pawley,
Chiara Lubich, Eli Folonari*

Speaking with Cardinal Tisserant in the Vatican, 1970

Giordani and his wife leaving the Quirinal Palace after an official reception, 1970

With Chiara Lubich at the Mariapolis Centre, Rocca di Papa, 1972

With Fr Pasquale Foresi when visiting Loppiano

Editor of Città Nuova, 1975: on the far left is Spartaco Lucarini, in the centre Guglielmo Boselli

With some gen 3 in Loppiano, 1976

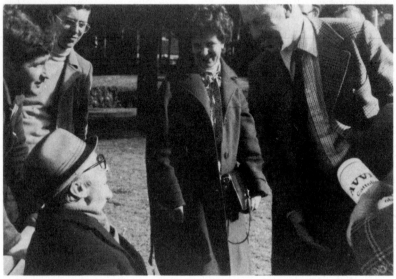

With some volunteers in the grounds of the Mariapolis Centre, Rocca di Papa

With some married focolarini in Loppiano, 1978

Celebrating his 80th birthday in the Mariapolis Centre, Rocca di Papa, 1974: on the left is Antonio Petrilli

The changing face of Igino Giordani as the years passed by . . .

Popolare Italiano. Don Sturzo had said that it should not oppose the Church, but remain separate – not a Church Party, but a Party favourable to the Church. The loyalties of a devout Catholic should never be challenged by loyalty to a political party. The Church could not be a party, because it was Catholic, ie. universal. But it was the task of the laity in particular to translate the Gospel into laws, institutions and customs, at the political, cultural and economic levels. The Church incarnates the Gospel, but it cannot be confused with a category (party or regime). As the Mystical Body of Christ it must love all, serve all, even the enemies of the Church. For this reason, it would be wrong to constitute a Catholic Party, because that would carry the danger of reducing Catholicism to a sect. Much of this is contained in the book already mentioned as Giordani's first important book, 'The Sign of Contradiction'. Giordani saw the real danger of identifying the Church with the Christian Democrats (DC). It was a logical step to agree that the Church needed a paper other than the organ of the DC: 'Il Quotidiano' as well as 'Il Popolo'.

In his autobiography, Giordani writes:

> The period of resistance, repression and study awakened in me again the ideals of the *Partito Popolare*, ie. the translation into politics of the ethics and even the theology of Christianity.*

With such sentiments, he discussed with Monsignor G.B. Montini, the formation of a party to do all these things, without having 'religious' or 'Catholic' in its title. Such a party would attract a wide range of people who had Christian values. So that, opposed to parties representing atheist dogmas and social ethics, anathema to the Church, there would be a party, broadly based, representing the

* *'Memorie'*, p.103.

Christians. Montini replied that such a party had been formed in Milan, *Democrazia Cristiana* (DC) and suggested that the PPI should merge with it to form a new DC which would serve, not the Church but the people, so gravely afflicted by civil war. Such a party must launch itself upon a programme of social justice and peace.

In 1944, Montini was appointed Papal Secretary of State and he recalled the discussion with Giordani. They had much in common. The new Secretary of State, almost immediately called upon Giordani to become director of a Catholic paper, not bound to any political party, to be called 'Il Quotidiano' and whose first issue, however modest, should appear on the day of Liberation, to carry the voice of the Church to the people. Iginio responded with a will. It was an apostolic directive. He mobilized his librarians to become journalists. Only De Gasperi was difficult as we have already seen. He had broken his ties with the Vatican Library and was established in the *Propaganda Fide* palace by the Spanish steps. He had prepared a paper for the DC and was all ready to go. This new paper seemed to offer undesirable competition. There would not be room for both 'Il Popolo' and 'Il Quotidiano'. Giordani saw that the Church needed its own paper and he wrote to De Gasperi, assuring him that while 'Il Quotidiano' would not always be uncritical, he could count upon it usually to support DC. Whether Giordani was right in assuming that there was room for two such similar papers, Rome in fact had three:

'Il Popolo', the organ of the *Democrazia Cristiana*;
'Il Quotidiano', the organ of faithful Christian laymen regardless of party;
'L'Osservatore Romano', the organ of the Church.

The offices of 'Il Quotidiano' were modest, two rooms attached to a stationery shop, in Via del Corso near to the Church of San Carlo.

There were three or sometimes four editors, but no correspondents outside Rome. The source of his inspiration in writing about social issues and Christian values was most clearly seen in his profound study of the Fathers.

The revolutionary

In his autobiography, Giordani tells of a day when he was summoned to talk with Pope Pius XII whom he knew well. He set off with expectations of a chat with an old friend – Papa Pacelli, whose biography he was later to write. On this occasion, Giordani records the conversation:

Pope: Giordani! What have you written in your newspaper? There have been complaints . . . they say you are a revolutionary: (The Pope then read a quote from a recent issue.) 'More from the rich and less from the poor. Property unjustly held and unjustly used is theft'.

Giordani: Holy Father, it is a quote from St. John Chrysostom.

Pope: Yes, I know, but do you have to use it? It isn't quite accurate!

Giordani: Holy Father, when you have to throw off an article in half an hour, or even an hour, you don't have time to check up all your references or spend time in bibliographical research.

Pope: True! True! (then turning to smile) They say that you are a revolutionary, but don't worry. You are in good company. They say that I am one too!

(In fact, Roosevelt had spoken of the Pope as being a radical.)

Giordani: But a true Christian is surely bound to be a revolutionary, is he not? Only his revolution does not wish to break up the world, but build it up, to bring love instead of hatred and to restore social solidarity.*

* ibid. p.105.

In these few months after the liberation Giordani was irrepressible. He had exactly the task he needed: his own paper and the mandate to be the voice of the Church, not the hierarchy, but the people of God, the laity:

> The first year of journalism in freedom, made me see that the Church was courted by not a few wealthy men only as a guardian of safes. In the first few months I was approached by some rich men but soon I was turned away by most of them, because I did not understand (with my usual 'naivety') the allusions in their conversation at the table and I just went on undaunted to carry out in the paper the social teaching of the Church. They had at first made vague promises of generous financial help to the newspaper; in the end they cut me off completely. The dilemma remained: to serve either God or Mammon.*

* ibid. p.106.

9

Giordani in his Fifties

Igino Giordani celebrated his 50th birthday 24th Sept 1944 with the war virtually ended and Rome already in the hands of the Allies. It was still a time of struggle and privation in Italy, but he had good reason to be satisfied that he had lived through a most disastrous war, honourably, usefully and without serious loss.

To an impartial observer, he would seem to be set for a brilliant political career and was, by his written word, a powerful influence in the building up of the moral stature of the land. He had apparently succeeded, often against considerable opposition, in every aspect of his life. His integrity was unquestioned and his record was clean. His defence of De Gasperi in the early days of Fascism had shown that from the beginning he understood the methods, the dangers and the evils of Fascism.

When I talk with people of his generation in Italy, I am constantly told that it was impossible to recognize what Fascism really stood for in the early days. I heard the same in Germany about Nazis. Igino Giordani was aware from the beginning of what he was dealing with. In this he was comparable to Dietrich Bonhoeffer in Germany. His role as protector of endangered politicians when he was head of the cataloguing section of the Vatican Library and his faithful editing and sometimes writing of 'Fides' showed him in 1944 to be the kind of man that Italy needed in its leadership. As editor of 'Il Quotidiano', he wielded an influence on behalf of the Church which could have considerable political importance. He was known to be no man's tool and his articles were feared by those whose motives he exposed. But he was not ambitious for a political career. He went into politics and accepted those responsibilities thrust upon him, but his heart was elsewhere.

The Diary

This can best be illustrated by quotations from his Diary, from May to October 1944. They show little concern with political intrigue, but much with spiritual and moral growth:

5th May – These last years, or days, have been given to us that we may witness our physical disintegration and attend to our moral edification; that we may realize the flimsiness of the world's structures and turn our hearts to the City of God. Illnesses, bereavements, collapses, hunger . . . the birthpangs of the soul which is being born to eternity.

17th August – Faith resolves suffering into love. Everything is resolved in love, in Christianity, which is an unceasing production of love. The Christian struggle for life is a continual defensive action to prevent love being overpowered.

18th October – Every day that is born is, as they say, a drawing nearer to death. And instead it is a drawing nearer to life, a tiresome extricating of oneself from this prison of death.

29th October – However well prepared you may be by historical studies, the bitterest surprise for you, now, is this: that in your doing of good you are misunderstood by the good, that in defence of religion you find yourself at odds with religious people: in order that your good may be wholly between you and

God, and no human praise or, worse, earthly reward
may be interposed.*

The Catholic politician

On the eve of his 50th birthday, Giordani had produced
a newspaper to be on the streets when Rome was
liberated. War-torn Europe faced real dangers of
chaos. The Allied Nations, now called the United
Nations, with some hope of permanent efforts for
peace, had concentrated upon defeating the Dictators
and the Fascist powers. But while the Allies were
united in their opposition to the common enemy they
had little else to hold them together. Soon Europe was
divided by an 'iron curtain', which ran through Germany and might have run through a divided Italy. It
nearly divided Austria and in Scandinavia, for a time,
Finland did not know which side it was on. Spain and
Portugal had kept out of the war and remained uncertain as to what their future would be. They were
eventually left alone, but the rest of Europe faced an
uncertain future. There was no natural successor to
Fascism in Italy. It could have been Communism.

The countries of Eastern Europe – within the Soviet
sphere of influence chose or were chosen for Communism. Alternative parties were not possible. In Western
Germany and Italy, Nazism and Fascism were not
permitted, but all else was possible. The Church had to
support an alternative and there was no Church Party
in Italy. The natural party was that of Don Sturzo, who
was still in exile. His successors were Alcide De
Gasperi and Igino Giordani. The Christian Democrats

* 'Diary of Fire', op. cit., p.20f..

seemed to be the heirs to Don Sturzo's party (the old PPI). As in the days of Don Sturzo, the party had to command the support of the Church, without being controlled by it. The two newspapers, 'Il Popolo' (Christian Democrat) and 'Il Quotidiano' (Church), represented the alternative emphases of De Gasperi and Giordani. But within a very short time, Giordani was directing 'Il Popolo'. To this day, it bears the mark of that struggle. The sub-title to 'Il Popolo' reads, *'Quotidiano della Democrazia Cristiana'*, which simply means 'the daily of the Christian Democrats', but imperceptibly it retains the name of the old Church Paper. The principles of the party to which both De Gasperi and Giordani belonged were basically the same as those of Don Sturzo's PPI.

After Fascism it had to be a different kind of party, simply because the isolation from which the Catholics were emerging this time was quite different. Those Catholics who had supported Fascism as well as those who had opposed it needed a new rallying point. Other parties had an advantage in their unity of experience. The Communists had an unbroken record of opposition to Fascism and they had their martyrs to show. The Socialist Party also bid for the anti-Fascist vote. Could the PPI reclaim the ground they had lost? There is no doubt that in the early days of Fascism they had shown a strong resistance and in that Giordani played his part. But the remnants of the PPI or the incipient DC had not been at the barricades. They could be interpreted as hiding or at least sheltering in the Vatican Library. It was the articles that Giordani had so persistently written against Fascism and De Gasperi's experience that had made it possible for them to take the field against Communists and Socialists. Giordani did much through 'Il Quotidiano' to show that the Church represented a force intact, capable of forming an alternative to Communism. But he still saw the need for a Christian and Catholic party rather than a Church party.

The Constitution

In 1946, Giordani was elected to the Constituent Assembly, which would have the responsibility of deciding upon the Constitution. As in Germany, a new constitution had to be drafted and accepted by a democratically elected Parliament before the Allied forces who held power would hand over. One big issue was whether Italy should be a Republic or a Monarchy. In the 1946 Constituent Assembly, the Christian Democrats had 207 of the 556 seats. This was not an overall majority, but they were by far the largest party. The other two major parties were Communists, 104; Socialists, 115.

Peter Nichols, in his very perceptive book, *'Italia, Italia',* has a description of the Christian Democratic Party and its importance since the war which is worth quoting at this point:

> The party is by far the most remarkable as well as the most powerful element in Italian politics. It is a post-war creation which took its name from a party formed at the end of the 19th century by left-wing Catholics, which was distrusted and finally suppressed by the Vatican but actually suppressed (along with all political parties) by Mussolini. It was refounded after the war with no clear idea of what it should be except to keep the Communists at bay, but like so many impromptu creations it has become the most important political instrument in the country and is fully supported by the Church. *

* Peter Nichols, *'Italia, Italia',* MacMillan, London, 1973, p.119f..

It is not difficult to see how reluctantly Giordani entered into this kind of political life.

Pietro Campitelli had persuaded Giordani to stand as a deputy for the Constituent Assembly. He consulted Monsignor Montini and, having obtained permission, gave up his direction of 'Il Quotidiano' and accepted this new honour, *'con scarsa convinzione'* (without much conviction), as he said. The Christian Democrat victory has been explained by many different theories. Was it all the Italian relatives writing from America? Was it a fear of passing over into the Eastern bloc with the Communists? Most likely it was because the leaders of the PPI had stayed in Italy. They had not been heroes – but they had got on with their ordinary lives as best they could under Fascism. The Church too seemed to be the only stable structure left which the ordinary man and even more the ordinary woman could recognize after the war as good.

The question of Republic or Monarchy was settled by referendum. For various reasons, King Victor Emmanuel III abdicated in favour of his son, Umberto. The referendum was held shortly after the Christian Democrat victory and the result was in favour of a Republic: 12,717,923 for a Republic; 10,719,284 for a Monarchy. Umberto abdicated on 13th June 1946. The vote was not overwhelming and no doubt most of the Christian Democrats voted for the Monarchy. But Igino Giordani was not among them. He saw the need for a Republic of Italy and a revision of political life. He was disappointed that the DC were as corrupt as many a pre-war party. Although he did his duty, he was without enthusiasm for political life. His own spiritual life, the defence of moral standards, his writing and his Church were of more importance to him than political success. He did none of those things that would have made him popular. He disliked demagogy. He knew that he would lose many

Catholic votes because he expressed his opinion that Italy should be a Republic. Yet, he made no secret of his views. A shrewd politician would have been ambiguous on such a controversial issue.

Giordani was obviously being consulted by many people who were in doubt about the relationship of their faith to their political allegiance and already it seems he was regarded as lay leader of Catholics in politics. He was rightly thought to have the ear of the hierarchy. Umberto Nobile, for example, consulted him in April 1946 to discuss his own dilemma. Umberto Nobile was a national hero for his voyage over the North Pole in a dirigible aircraft. But his anti-Fascist enthusiasm had carried him away to the extent of allowing his famous name to be used by the Communists in their list. He came to Giordani as to a priest asking about the effect that would have upon his faith.

In December of that year, Giordani heard from Don Sturzo in America by means of a confidential letter to Monsignor Montini. Don Sturzo had agreed to take no part in politics during his exile, but he was now about to break his silence. A few days later there was news that Don Sturzo had strongly condemned the peace treaty which the Allies had with Italy.

The first Parliament

After the Constituent Assembly had done its job and the referendum had been held which declared Italy a Republic, a new Parliament had to be elected. Giordani was elected to this in 1948. It had been an even greater success for the Christian Democrats than the first election. This time they had an overall majority – 305 in a Parliament of

574. Communists and Socialists between them had only mustered 183 seats. Giordani was all set for a successful political career, but his heart was not in it. He was prepared to do his duty for his country, but the role of a politician was not his. Malcolm Muggeridge wrote somewhere that 'the children of light' have no place in politics – at least not successfully. Giordani was undoubtedly one of the 'children of light' and his principles as well as his high integrity made politics with all its compromises almost impossible for him.

An example of this was shown shortly after the election when a crisis arose about the choice of ministers for the new government. Changes were always being made to compensate one or other member for services rendered and Giordani, heartily sick of the dealings, stayed away from the meeting. De Gasperi asked him later in surprise why he had not been there. De Gasperi had wanted him for Under Secretary for Cultural Relations in Foreign Affairs. It would have been a good choice, but Giordani was not prepared to go through the process by which he could buy his place. The little corruption which is necessary to make an Italian government work was too much for the high morals of Igino Giordani.

Travel

The first years of re-entry into political life were for Giordani, years of travel. He was invited to London to participate in a Congress of Catholic Action. He met Stafford Cripps, Cardinal Heenan, the Archbishop of Canterbury, Lord Halifax and other notables. He spoke in the Albert Hall.

He accepted an invitation to speak in Spain in 1948 on

the occasion of celebrations for Jaimes Balmes and in France where he met Gilson and Aron. Although elected to the Council of the Commune of Rome in 1948, he appears to have been much involved in travel and other activities. Of course, he had to resign from the Council when he became a Deputy again in the 1948 election. That same year, much involved with the DC, he took charge of 'Il Popolo'. It was therefore a very important figure that Moral Rearmament captured for a visit to their centre at Caux above Montreux. Mya was able to go with him on this visit to Switzerland. Many of the leading political figures in Europe found their way to the hospitality of MRA at Caux and it is not difficult to see how its direct message of absolute standards made its appeal to Igino Giordani. If the MRA theory that you can put the world right by putting the individual right were true, Giordani should be a good illustration.

16th March 1949

A change took place in Giordani while he was a deputy in the 1948 Parliament. He was more spiritually aware. The MRA might have put it down to contacts they had made with him in Caux; those who met him in England, Spain and France, may have put it down to his wider vision as he moved out of the isolation of Italy. It is now clear that in meeting Chiara Lubich he found what he had been searching for all his life and found his place in the Church – no longer a spiritual proletariat! The new confidence enabled him to see more clearly than he had ever seen before what was happening to the post-war world.
He saw the divisions between east and west, not as ideological positions, between Communism and Capitalism,

but as dangerous imperial divisions between two potential bidders for world domination.

The occasion of his greatest speech in Parliament and the one that meant the end of his political career was a debate on the Atlantic Treaty. This was the basis of NATO and put Italy firmly into the western bloc, giving her a part in the organization which kept two armed halves of the world facing each other. Giordani spoke for an hour in that debate – 11.30 to 12.30 on 16th March 1949. The North Atlantic Treaty Organization was presented purely as an anti-Communist force designed to prevent world Communism from assuming a dominance or any undue influence in that part of the world that was designated as western sphere of influence. Giordani knew that Italy had a large Communist party. It was almost the accepted Opposition. To regard it only as the enemy would be to divide Italy dangerously. NATO was also a group of armed forces which existed to warn and threaten Russia. At that time, America had the atomic bomb and western world dominance was by no means impossible. McCarthyism was growing in the USA, and Giordani did not like what he saw.

It was a stormy speech which took courage to deliver. He resisted the accusation of Togliatti, the Communist leader, who had described the DC as a 'Catholic' party, with his usual argument that 'Catholic' means 'universal' and cannot be a party. He went on to say that every war is a failure of Christianity. 'If the world were Christian, there would be no need of war'.* He cleared himself of communist sympathies when he turned to Togliatti and said: 'You condemn war made by anti-communists, but applaud war made in China for Communists'.†

* *'Memorie'*, p.111.
† ibid..

When another member of the Communist Party, Longo, insisted that it was a war of liberation he drew upon his full polemic style with: 'I have never heard anyone say they were making war because they were cruel or foolish. Everybody who makes war says he does it for justice'.* And that argument was used as strongly against NATO 'War – in addition – is a homicide, a deicide (God is killed in effigy: in man who is his image) and a suicide'.† Togliatti hardly knew where he stood. Sometimes he interrupted to contradict; sometimes to applaud and agree, because this was a time when 'peace' was a communist slogan. Giordani argued for peace and he was against Italy joining any bloc that might lead to a third world war between America and Russia which he saw as a possible atomic war.

The long speech was applauded by left and right. It was also heavily criticized. De Gasperi did not applaud. Giordani had sacrificed his political career. He continued as deputy until the next election which was in 1953, but he sought no office. He had been director of 'Il Popolo' since August 1946 and he used the paper to publish a summary of his speech under the title 'No to War'.

In his travels after the famous speech, he spoke insistently and consistently about peace. The Communists thought they saw an ally and invited him to the Soviet Union, but he refused the invitation because of the interpretation that must be put upon it. He saw that they wanted to use his name.

The withdrawal from politics

He had entered Parliament, *'con scarsa convinzione'*, and he had done his duty. No party could really hold this man of

* ibid..
† ibid..

conscience. He saw the dangers of war and of a divided world. He had a vision of Italy as a land of peace between warring nations and he threw all his skills into arguing for Italian neutrality. So long as he could help guide the direction of political life, he remained. Gradually he saw that it was a life for the ambitious and not for the idealists. He did not break with De Gasperi, and there were times when the Prime Minister envied his peace of conscience. He could not withdraw at once, because he was too heavily involved. He had a following in Parliament for his peace policy, although they were not all, or principally of his party. He was the most skilled political writer of his day and his pen was sought. Gradually his writing was less for 'Il Popolo' and more for 'La Via'. It was in the latter – a Catholic paper – that he put the issue of peace and war with its terrible alternatives most clearly in an article entitled 'War or Peace?'

But it was not only his dissatisfaction with politics which caused the change. It was a growing conviction that his vocation lay elsewhere. He saw that the renewal of the Church was a more effective way of saving the world than a renewal of politics. Perhaps it was because he was an Italian. The Italians have never believed the fantastic things they say about what governments can achieve. They have always known that there are institutions in society which are more effective for change than governments.

Intermezzo

The kindling of the fire: 17th September 1948

A week before his 54th birthday, Igino Giordani had an appointment in a meeting room of the Italian Parliament with a group of representatives from Religious Orders and Movements. He had had many such meetings, because he was the obvious deputy to go to if you wanted something from Parliament. One of the deputation was Chiara Lubich. She was 28, approaching her 29th birthday in the following January. Giordani was deeply impressed by her. Chiara is to this day the acknowledged founder of the Focolare Movement. Celibate laymen had joined the Movement that very year and it was growing outside of the northern Italian region of Trent. There was a glow of spirituality about them which at once attracted Giordani. He saw that they had more power to change Italy and the world than all the Italian governments.

Later on he said of the visit:

[Chiara Lubich] told the story of four or five young girls from Trent who met together with her during the war to live a life of dedication to God and of service to the suffering, while, with war raging all around them, everything was collapsing. The impression of what she told me is recorded in my diary, written that evening: 'Simplicity of the Gospel, atmosphere of Paradise. . . '*

---

* *Come conobbi i Focolari* (How I came to know the Focolare), art, in 'Città Nuova', no.9, 1980, p.44.

145

Giordani becomes a focolarino

It was a very simple operation. In many ways, Giordani had been prepared for this Movement. He was a spiritually minded man and as such a little out of his element in politics. He was a patristic scholar who sought to apply the teaching of the Early Church to life in Italy today. He was a distinguished writer, but the best of his writings were about the life of a Christian in the world. He had reached the point when he knew that the political chapter of his life must soon close. All his life he had sought for Saint Catherine of Siena and there before him in that little group was the one he sought. It is surprising how close the spirituality of Chiara is to that of St. Catherine. And this Movement of hers was for unity. He had sought unity all his life and here he found in his own Church a gift from God to a spiritual being who knew that she was chosen for unity. It did not take either of them long to discover that they needed each other.

A week later, on his birthday, Igino wrote in his diary:

24th September – There is no need, Lord, for me to tell over again the catalogue of my needs, endless as it is.

It is enough that I need you.*

Something of the same spirituality was to be found in Chiara. Only a few years before, when she was still in the midst of the bombing of Trent, Elena Molignoni, a girl from Castello where she used to teach, appealed to her to come to the safety of the countryside. She replied that it was a privilege to suffer and that whether she lived or died she would praise God. Then came that flash of spiritual insight, so typical of Chiara and so appealing to Igino:

Think Elena, *we are able to love God with this little heart!* We

* 'Diary of Fire', op. cit., p.38.

146

are able to love God! Nothing, nothing can take this love away, not even the worst of bombardments.*

I have dealt at length with the 'spirituality' of Chiara Lubich in my book, 'Chiara',† and in this present book I have tried to follow the progress of the rich spiritual life of Igino Giordani. A careful study of these two kinds of spirituality, each nurtured in different soils, shows a close resemblance. It would be difficult to find life-experiences more different than those of Chiara and Igino. But it is remarkable how they were prepared for each other. That September day in 1948 was a meeting point of God's plans for two of his children. Chiara was opening like a flower, her Movement still unaware of its great spiritual potential; Igino was at the end of a political career which he could only re-enter at the cost of compromise, he was at the beginning of a new sense of the unity of the Church. Chiara needed the assurance that she could take her flower out into the world. He saw in this Movement something he had sought long. The spiritual quality of Chiara had enabled her to go beyond the accepted orders; the lay and married status of Igino was accepted at its spiritual level and not reduced to the proletariat. It was not only a celibate priest who could be holy. A woman could be holy; a married man could be holy.

The offer and the acceptance

Igino Giordani's first meeting with Chiara Lubich convinced him of the importance of the Focolare Movement, an importance which he saw more clearly than she did. It was he who urged her to move outwards. He realized the

* 'Chiara', op. cit., p.21.
† op. cit..

147

enormous potential of this Movement which had come from her charism of unity. On one of his visits to the women's focolare over which Chiara presided, he spoke of 'virginity' with such eloquence and respect for its virtue, that Chiara was deeply impressed by his humility. Here was a man who praised a virtue from which he was excluded. She replied in her good direct style that what counts is charity and that there were many proud virgins who may well be in hell for their pride.

In various meetings and discussions, a relationship of mutual respect grew up between Igino and Chiara. Giordani had to travel much in his work and whenever he could he routed himself through Trent. With that impish smile, he explained to me that wherever he travelled, he found that the route was through Trent! 'From Rome to Paris, I went by way of Trent; I even found that from Rome to Naples was by way of Trent'.

That relationship was more than personal: it strengthened the whole Movement and allowed it to open up to the world and the problems of society. When Giordani asked if he could be a focolarino, she did not hesitate to say 'yes!' even though that would have revolutionary consequences for the Movement. Her unhesitating reply was typical. Somehow, she had anticipated all the future unfolding of the Movement even when she did not fully understand what that would mean. You can catch a glimpse of that early relationship, with its naturalness and openness in the record of the conversation as it was later recorded by Giordani in an interview:

> 'Couldn't I be part of your community?' I asked. 'Why not?' was the answer. 'We want to be Christians as the Church wants us to be: to bear witness to Christ, that's all. You can do it too: come and join us.'*

* Lorit and Grimaldi, op. cit., p.56

And Giordani became the first married focolarino. He carried on living with his family, but was fully part of the new community. He brought with him all his rich experience of working with the laity of the Church, and he soon discovered that the step he had taken gave a new breadth to the Movement. He also recognized that he had found the status in the Christian community for himself and others like him that he had long sought: 'The presence of a married man (and of a politician at that!) in the Focolare meant that the label of outsider no longer applied to someone belonging to a part of society which was commonly excluded from a life of virtue!'*

As he said years later:

I found a new purpose for my Christian life, so far as my being married was concerned. As I have said, I felt part of the proletariat of Christianity, an outsider. But now, by means of this life in common, I was together with celibates, together with priests, together with the whole Church. Their treasures, their contemplation, their virtues, became my possessions too, and I shared my sufferings with them – it became a whole life and the whole of life became beautiful. Holiness henceforth was not something distant from us and foreign. Contemplation itself could be our very own.†

A new name

Among the many sayings of Jesus, not included in the Gospels, but quoted by writers in the Early Church (some even quoted within the New Testament) is one which we owe to Origen: 'I have read somewhere', he writes, 'what purports to be an utterance of the Saviour, and wonder

* ibid. p.57
† *Come conobbi i Focolari*, art, cit., p.44.

whether someone put it into the mouth of the Saviour or someone remembered it, "He who is near me is near the fire; he who is far from me is far from the kingdom" '.

In his mind, Igino had taken to calling Chiara 'the fire' (in Italian, *fuoco*). But Chiara had been thinking on much the same lines, and it was she who first voiced her thoughts. She called him 'Foco' and that became his name in the Focolare Moment. As she wrote after his death:

> He personified the *nom de guerre* by which he was known in the Movement: Foco, fire, meaning the supernatural and natural love for God and one's neighbour, which is the basis and the summit of Christian life. And he contributed in a unique way to keep alive among all of us the 'Word of Life' which had been given to him on his entry into the Movement: 'Love one another as I have loved you' – a word that he seems now to leave to all of us as a final exhortation and his testament.*

Chiara Lubich

What do we know of this woman who so influenced Igino Giordani or of the Movement that opened up a new world to him? We shall deal with the Movement in Part II of this book because after this meeting in 1948, the life of Igino was bound up with the Movement. But what of Chiara Lubich? In 1977, she was awarded the Templeton Prize for 'Progress in Religion'. We must look briefly at her life up to this point if we are to understand the impact she made upon Igino Giordani.

She was born in Trent, 22nd January 1920, baptized there as Silvia, trained as a teacher in the war years and active in Catholic Action when she taught in the rural

---

* *Igino Giordani, focolarino,* art in 'Città Nuova', no.9, 1980, p.22.

areas of Trentino. She took the name of Chiara when she became a tertiary of the Franciscan Order. As a school-girl, she had gone to Loreto with Catholic Action and been deeply impressed by the little house which purports to be the house where Jesus was brought up in Nazareth, brought to Loreto by angels. She was not interested in the discussions about authenticity, but heard the voices of Jesus and Mary in that little house as she meditated. She returned from Loreto with a sure knowledge of her vocation not to marriage, not to a convent, not to a celibate life in the world. She knew there was a fourth way. She committed herself to God as a celibate member of a true family in the world. From her has come the basic idea of celibates living in families and working in the world. The focolare is as much a family of love as any family. Her inspiration was to live the Gospel in the world.

The first band of young girls she gathered round her were devout Catholic girls who pledged themselves to one another in love in the air-raid shelters of Trent. They read the Gospels and tried to live them. A verse stands out in their experience: 'Where two or three are gathered together in my name, there am I in the midst of them'. (Matt. 18:20) They talked of putting Jesus in the midst when they came together.

The whole Gospel emerged in their lives and they lived it consciously and deliberately in the world. They read the Gospel better than the most erudite scholar.

The Movement was only a few years old when Chiara met Igino Giordani in 1948, but already it was spreading beyond Trent and Chiara was opening a focolare in Rome. This rapid development in so short a time was one of the things that impressed Giordani.

But perhaps we should let Chiara say it in her own words:

He was the one who opened the doors of the focolare to married people. They followed him in his desire for sanctity and consecration. In this way, something which had at first been only dimly foreseen, became a reality – virgins and married people could follow, insofar as it is possible, the same way, living after the model of the family of Nazareth.*

The most decisive event in his life

That is what Domenico Mondrone calls it in, *'I santi ci sono ancora'* ('The Saints are Still with Us')† The first of the collection in that volume is Igino Giordani. In one section which bears the same heading as this paragraph, the Jesuit writer assesses Giordani's preparedness for this encounter with Chiara. I will quote at length from that section:

> But in the life of Igino Giordani, about half way along the road, there was an encounter which completely shatterred his whole being, launching him into a new and unanticipated world, but for which he had, in fact, been prepared, if you include immediate awareness and total involvement. He found there such a fullness of life, which he described many years later, 'Now in the focolare, I am living my true youth'.
>
> His contacts with the saints – and he had studied and written about all kinds and conditions – must have engraved upon his soul an integrity and purity. A nostalgia for holiness was like leaven in his life, but he had not succeeded in opening the way. He had loved his family as 'a reality which incarnates on earth the ideal of the divine-human love'. He had learnt to love the Church with the passion of a son; he had given the best years of his life to it. In this, the meetings with Mother Oliva

* Art. in 'Living City', New York, July 1980, p.7.
† Section entitled 'Igino Giordani', Edizione Pro Sanctitate, Rome, 1980, Vol. VI.

Bonaldo, the founder of 'The Daughters of the Church', had been of great help. But there was always something lacking and he felt this deep down: there was always a great emptiness to be filled, and he searched and searched. It was like something gnawing at him and tormenting him.

The Lord had created in him the conditions necessary for him to be susceptible to an encounter which he was preparing for him. Two years after the war, he was a deputy in the Italian Parliament. From time to time, he heard talk of a Movement coming out of Trent led by a woman who wanted to make something of this shattered world. It wasn't the first time such news had come to him; he could usually shrug his sholders and forget about it. One day in 1948 when he was librarian of the Parliament, three religious asked for an audience – a Friar Minor, a Conventural and a Capuchin – and with them two tertiaries of the Franciscan Order, one woman and one man. He was struck that something should have reconciled these hostile children of St. Francis! The woman was Chiara Lubich and it was she who, in an audience of only a few minutes, explained the object of the visit. She did not deliver a 'sermon', but put forward a most serious and concrete proposal.

This was just the first of a whole series of contacts that Igino Giordani would have with her. He understood at once that he had met something very important . . . Igino Giordani, who had read and studied much, who had been enriched by a great variety of cultures, who up to that point had profited from the experience of being a master, saw himself in that first instant as if before a miracle, and felt like a new boy at school. In his humility he had to admit that this young girl knew more than he did. She had read the Gospel better.★

Giordani's words put this quite simply. 'I began to understand life, I began to understand love. I saw creatures who loved as children of God must love'.

His meeting with Chiara, then, touched the whole of

★ ibid. pp. 25-27, 30.

his being and prepared the way for the discovery of his vocation. When, after this encounter, Giordani became 'Foco' it was not a simple change of name, but a leap ahead in his spiritual life.

Part Two

The Focolare
Movement

1

A New Spirituality

In 1948, Igino Giordani met, not a movement, but Chiara. This remarkable woman from Trent impressed him by her directness. She did not talk a pious language, but came directly to the point. She was filled with a love for God and for her fellows which did not need to be buttressed by quotations. She marvelled at God's love for her and for all his creatures; but there was one greater wonder: she never questioned her belief in God, she marvelled at his great and beautiful power in the world, she obeyed him quite naturally. The sheer wonder of it possessed her soul.

When one stormy morning in Trent, she went through the darkness to the church where she would make her vows, the doors seemed to open of their own accord, like the stone rolled away on Easter morning, or as she put it, like the arms of God open to embrace her. God was the beginning and the end and the way for her. She saw her love for God, as she saw much else, in triangular form: God, herself and her neighbour. God always took the initiative – when you think you are dealing with God, he is dealing with you. 'We love because he first loved us'. Our love burns like little flames, but left alone these flames will go out. They are fuelled by one another and all are fuelled by God. The imagery is rich and full, but it is not remote.

And what was new?

Giordani had heard it all before. She quoted the Fathers, but he had read more texts than she had and written in many books the very things she was saying. Chiara was orthodox in everything. But there *was* something else. 'She read the Gospels better than I did'. Even more important was his comment that her friends seemed 'to love like children of God'. It was the quality of their love.

Perhaps the only answer to the question 'And what was new?' is to draw an analogy with human love. Every lover knows that his or her love is like no other love the world has ever known, although many millions have loved before. Love cannot tolerate the thought that it is not unique. Chiara was not the first to love God with her whole being, but her love was unique because it really was hers. She was not learning the art of love from someone else and then practising it perfectly. It was a direct love, in no way derivative. Giordani recognized this and later he would see the full force of her own explanation:

> God, the most holy and blessed Trinity, appeared like the sun at the dawn of a world that was rediscovering peace after the pandemonium of war; and he offered to us, his children, a more divine life than the already good life that some of us were leading, he offered us a more consistently Christian life, a more integral life.*

If St. Francis had asked Chiara 'Little daughter, what do you want?' she too would have replied, without prompting, 'God'.

* 'May They All Be One', New City, London, 1977, p.22.

Saint Catherine of Siena

Igino could hear again the sentiments of St. Catherine in the things that Chiara was describing. It is enough to quote from Father Kenelm Foster, O.P., in his *'Introduction'* to 'I, Catherine', a description of the young Catherine, to see the similarity:

> The slender figure in the white tunic and the blue mantle, going around on errands of mercy, began to be talked about. Some professed to be shocked by the freedom of her ways (she always, we are told, looked you in the eyes when she spoke); and her austerities, which she could hardly keep concealed, were criticized by the wise and prudent. But many were drawn to her, and not only by her cheerful goodness but also increasingly by her intelligence. She did not seek to be loved, but to love; but her Dominican training had not been wasted and she was already clear in her young mind that the way to love was through knowledge. This truth she had already tested in the matter of loving God; she now had to discover – for her a harder task – the loveableness of human beings. So, as usual, she turned to Christ and begged for the grace to 'perceive the beauty of all souls she came in contact with, so that she would be more prompt to work for their salvation.'*

There was no conscious modelling on the part of Chiara and of course the differences between the 14th and 20th centuries are bound to be evident, but the more you read the letters collected in 'I, Catherine', the more it becomes clear that what must have attracted Giordani to Chiara was at least partly the strong similarity to his favourite saint. This also comes out in their attitude to good and evil, because she related everything to God, the creative and creating God. Evil had to be recognized, but it was always the desecration of the goodness already

* Kenelm Foster, OP, 'I, Catherine', Collins, London, 1980, p.18.

bestowed, and it need never have happened. Or as T. Deman writes in a supplement to 'Vie Spirituelle.' 'According to current views, what needs explaining is how man ever does what is right; but as Catherine sees it, what needs explaining is how he can ever go wrong'.*

The spirituality of Chiara can more easily be related to that world before the Reformation than to anything that followed the major upheaval and division of the Church. That may be why she so readily bears the burden of unity. All parts of the Church can understand a spirituality which, while related most practically to the modern world, takes little or no account of divisions caused by the Reformation. This is immediately clear in her conversation with Protestants. Although she is a Catholic and most orthodox, she talks a language which takes no account of the divisions.

The presence of Christ

The love of God leads to a love for the world. The longing of Chiara is to do as Mary has done – to give Christ to the world. Her spirituality sees Christ present in the world in six different ways:

1. Jesus in the midst – 'where two or three are gathered together in my name, there am I in the midst of them'.
2. Jesus in the Eucharist – 'this is my body broken for you'
3. Jesus in his word – 'if you continue in my word, you are truly my disciples'.
4. Jesus in our brother – 'inasmuch as you have done

* Art. in 'Vie Spirituelle', October 1934, p.11, quoted in Kenelm Foster, op. cit., p.18.

it unto the least of these my brothers, you have done it unto me'.

5. Jesus in the hierarchy – 'he who hears you hears me'.

6. Jesus in me – if I listen to the voice of the Spirit who speaks 'within'.

The awareness of Christ present is based upon the experience of life and adherence to the Scriptures. The life which Chiara was developing in the Focolare Movement was no more than the authentic life of a Christian in the world. To this day, the Eucharist is of particlar importance for her followers. When a focolare comes to a new locality the first impact the group makes is that of a faithful attendance at the Eucharist. Equally in their personal lives, lived together, the need to 'put Jesus in the midst' is paramount. There are many stories told by Chiara herself, even one from the very first focolare, of difficulties that are resolved by coming together and putting Jesus in the midst by their mutual love.

Chiara tells of one experience of loneliness and darkness in a situation of imperfect love among her companions, which ends with these words:

> And I decided to wait for my friends in order to put Jesus back in our midst in order to see again. And that's what happened.
>
> In being united . . . we felt the strength of Jesus among us.*

Love like fire rises to the heights

A few weeks before he met Chiara, Igino Giordani entered in his diary for *5th August 1948:*

* 'Where Two or Three', New City, London, 1977, p.24.

All these clamours, from political meetings and assemblies, all this frenzy of ambitions and intrigues, all these anxieties over disasters and over trifles, will sink into silence, wrapped in darkness, as soon as death comes . . . The antipathies by which we are torn, the ideologies for which we disquiet ourselves, the impostures and the conventions, the rhetoric and the treachery, all will collapse into nothing, dissolving, in an instant into nought; hell will be the great rubbish dump where all those forms of evildoing will be heaped up, and where they will ferment into gases poisonous to the soul which, at least in death, has not freed itself in God.*

It is not difficult to trace in those words the pain that Igino Giordani had suffered in all the intrigues of politics with which he had been involved in those post-war years. He was remembered by his colleagues as a man of integrity, who hated the struggles for power. Not that he was soft – St. Catherine, his model, was not soft either. Hardened politicians feared to cross him in debate.

But he hated 'clamours, treachery and intrigues'. The next paragraph in that entry of August 5th continues with a note on that suffering:

And vice-versa, the sufferings, the humble sighs, the desires to do good, the loaves given with a smile to the poor, all the good deeds and reflexions carried out amidst the press of hatreds and hypocrisies, all this humble production of good through the miracle of death, will grow into eternal life, will mount into the light, will take on the breadth of the rainbow, drawing furrows of light across the immense purity of the heavens.†

Igino is lyrical even in his diary and after these two contrasting pictures, he writes about death in a way that shows deeply the spiritual attitude he has to his own death, which he had faced so many times in his life, and the longing for social justice about which he had so often

* 'Diary of Fire', op. cit., p.35f..
† ibid. p.36.

162

written. While other deputies in the Italian Parliament were jockeying for positions, he was contemplating divine justice:

> Thus death is the crisis which settles all: the violent shift of scene: a changing of the guard which reverses positions, since it brings into the kingdom of the anonymous crowds, feeble creatures, the unknown servants of the human family, the victims of sacrifice, people tried by suffering and love. It is the great act of justice, in which the screens and the curtains of wealth and imposture will be swept away by a burst of flame, laying bare the ugliness that has not been seen and at the same time the beauty that has gone unnoticed:*

That short meditation on death, the revealer of true values must be read against a growing disillusion with political life. It is followed by a few short paragraphs on love and humility which reveal how near he was to Chiara even before he met her:

> Love, like fire, tends to mount on high, eager to return to God . . . Flaming only towards the heights, to embrace all creatures, it must begin from the bottom: begin from ground level in order to soar towards the blue of the heavens . . . And since it is made concrete in service, in order to serve, it puts itself beneath the most abject human being, so that not even he may withdraw himself from the warmth of love.
>
> For this reason humility is needed, which is putting oneself on the *humus*, on the ground, upsetting all stools and footrests, and all the multifarious objects which enable one to get on top. The man who gets on top rejects someone or something: in that 'some person' there is a representation of God, something divine: so that the prouder a man becomes, that is, gets on top, the more he impoverishes himself. The saint's ambition does not reject anything: it tends to envelop in its love all creatures, like St. Francis.†

* ibid..
† ibid. p.36f..

At the time of writing, Igino was in line for high office. But his integrity and his very high standards made it difficult for him to compromise. Returning to that important 5th August entry, we detect the struggle:

Humility is a position of conquest, it belongs to the heroes of charity.

To put oneself beneath all: a condition for loving – serving – all.

A simplifying position, in which intrigues, pressures and quarrels have no play: the man who puts himself down there is left in peace, in the transparent atmosphere which precedes sin; the sin of worldly ambitions and of money, power and lust. Wickedness is mediocre: and it stays in mid-air: it does not reach heaven any more than it touches the earth: it has no height because it lacks a base. It is cessation from good. *

The search for goodness

We have seen how those in the corridors of power regarded Igino Giordani as an idealist and perhaps 'ingenuous'. The hard battles and compromises of political life strained his conscience and his search for goodness and virtue. He could not have allowed himself to do the things that other politicians did. If he ever considered taking the compromised position that led to power, he rebuked himself in his diary, which is remarkably frank. He called his draft autobiography, *'Memorie di un cristiano ingenuo'* ('Memoirs of an Igenuous Christian'), and when I asked if I might see his diary upon which much of his autobiography was based, he replied with that inimitable twinkle in his eyes: 'So you want to tell the world about all my horrible secrets'. And one of

* ibid. p.37.

164

these secrets was his wrestling with himself about the price to be paid for high office.

Spernere se, sperni (to despise oneself, to be despised). That is freedom. That is happiness. You on the other hand seek your reward here below; you do good in order to have the esteem of men; you cultivate virtue in order to be paid for it. You are worse than the pagans; you are the most wretched of traders.

The Christian is to be another Christ; and therefore you must expect spittle and derision and the judgement that puts you beneath the feet of a robber. You must be killed by the multitude amidst the cries of 'Long Live Barabbas!'

You are always looking for praise from outside: you live for it. It drains you, and it distracts you from your interior life, and keeps you absorbed in an anxious scheming to win applause and petty rewards. It keeps you in the fine dust of gossip, in the bustle of lobbies and chambers, in conferences and hotels. And so you lose yourself and you lose others. You are pulled apart by the wind that descends from the roofs, by the dust that swirls through the streets, by the death of which vain things are unceasingly dying.*

For years the politically experienced Igino Giordani had lived in the exile of the Vatican Library believing that he could play his part when Fascism had been destroyed. He believed in the role that good Catholics could play in the political life of Italy.

But his passionate search for virtue and his hatred of compromise raised serious questions about his political vocation. Even more, he was feeling the pull towards a spiritual vocation which did not correspond to any existing order. Neither the Chamber of Deputies nor the accepted orders within the Church provided the proper field for the vocation to which God was calling him.

But this search for virtue presented him with an

* ibid. p.37f..

165

agonizing decision – could he retain his vocation as a Catholic in the political intrigues and treacheries of the Chamber of Deputies. It was a decision similar to that which Chiara had to make when she returned from the blinding experience of Loreto and was faced with the traditional vocations of the Church. She decided to live in the world as part of a new family of totally committed people. Giordani did not leave politics, even after he met her, but he carried within him the struggle which was ultimately to lead him away from political power and towards 'consecration', which he had always sought.

One last quote from the diary on this theme. It is for 16th August, a month before meeting with Chiara Lubich:

> You cling to life as fiercely as if you were trying to have a quarter of it to live over again after your death, by binding yourself to memories, fame and gratitude. And you find that your time is overcast with clouds of fear: fears that the new invasions may submerge, along with Europe, your own titles to remembrance and gratitude, the things that are dear to you and the persons connected with you. And this thought, which is a possibility, brings home to you the precariousness of all: it is a lecture on the Imitation of Christ given from the chair of pestilence and explosives.*

As he wrote, the threat of Communism was real, the cold war had started and although the Christian Democrats were in power they had to make alliances to assure their continuance. The American influence was strong and both its money and the possession of the atomic bomb bred fear or confidence. It was in this atmosphere and with those thoughts confided to his diary that 17th September dawned. There is a freshness still about his entry for that day:

* ibid. p.38.

17 September – This morning, at Montecitorio, I was called upon by angels: a Capuchin, a Friar Minor, a Conventual Franciscan, a man and woman belonging to the Third Order: the woman was Silvia Lubig who is launching a community at Trent.*

We have described that meeting in full in the last chapter.

The word of life

A characteristic of the Focolare Movement is the 'word of life'. This is a text chosen every month for the whole Movement to use as their guide to life during that month. It can also be given to a member of the Movement as a life task.

As a focolarino, Giordani had his 'word of life', given to him a few years after he joined the Movement. But already in the early months, his powerful yearning for holiness developed into a more total and complete adherence to the plan of God which, having been recognized in him by Chiara, he considered as his 'word of life', 'Jesus I wish to be yours: yours as you think best: do with me all that you wish'. He records this in his diary on 27th February 1949 when he was at Tonadico in the Dolomites.

It is particularly interesting to see how appropriate this prayer was. I have frequently been impressed by such appropriateness in others. With Igino, we may trace in his 'Diary of Fire', the way in which his mind moves from September 1948, when he met Chiara, to February 1949, when he records this word given to him at Tonadico. A few quotes of entries written in the midst of travel and political activity will suffice.

* ibid..

167

[1948]: 24 October – If the spectacle of human meanness disquiets you, contemplate the majesty of God.

And if humanity appears ugly, restore your eyes by contemplating God.*

28 November – . . . I wish to offer my sufferings to Christ, enclosing them in silence with which I wish to counter cruel words. I wish to give love for hatred, forgiveness for revenge, intelligence for instinct: I will not let myself be overcome by the weakness of the violent.

Jesus said to the Blessed Angela of Foligno: 'You will know that I am in you when, if someone outrages and hurts you, you not only endure it with patience but also feel a lively desire for outrages and sufferings and consider them when they come as a grace. This is the most certain sign of God' (*The Wonderful Visions*).

True – and this is where *I* fall most easily and betray grace. Pride is an outward expansion to compensate for an inward contraction.

18 December – At 2.30 this morning I took an aeroplane of the Brazilian Pan Air Line at Ciampino [Rome] and after a flight of five hours I reached Lisbon, to which I had been invited by the newspaper *Novidades*. At Lisbon I spoke in the hall of the Geographical Society to an assembly of three thousand persons, including the Cardinal Patriarch and eighteen bishops. I spoke about Catholic journalism, in Portugese. The following morning I was at Fatima. Yesterday evening I had half an hour's conversation with Salazar, the Head of Government. Speaking of the governments of various European countries, he sagely concluded: 'Until the people grow tired of us'.

1949. 4 January – Lord, I ask you for health, intelligence, strength, wealth, love, satisfaction, a healthy family, happiness on earth and paradise in heaven: and in return I give you distractions, coldness, doubts, lies, compromises with lust and luxury, base passions, wretchedness and treachery . . .

30 January – . . . To die to the world, to die to oneself. The effect resembles physical death. Like it, it leads to a liberation from the daily assault of evil, it puts us beyond

*ibid..

its grasp; it liberates us. But not for a cessation of life, much rather for a completion of it; for God puts himself in the place of the ego and then life assumes giant proportions. Once God is in us who is against us?. . .

10 February – Yesterday in the Chamber of Deputies, I spoke on the occasion of the centenary of the Roman Republic and sketched a profile of Mazzini from the Catholic point of view. The subject was rather a difficult one for a Catholic but I received congratulations for my speech from Catholics, Republicans, Socialists and Monarchists.

27 February – Tonadico – I have been given this Word of Life: 'Jesus I wish to be yours as you think best; do with me all that you wish.'*

For more than 31 years, he loved that word. There is no trace in all the years that followed of a disappointed ex-politician. He was at peace. He might have held high office in the Italian Government, but that is not what he read to be the will of Jesus for him. Every decision taken in those years that were to elapse before he died in 1980 was taken consciously seeking the will of his Lord. And at the end the utter peace of obedience was in his heart.

* ibid. pp. 40–42

2

Early Contacts with the Focolare Movement

After the meeting with Chiara, Igino was still deeply involved in political affairs and was much in demand as a speaker. This took him to many parts of Europe, and as we indicated earlier, he took every opportunity of calling on Chiara in Trent. Her influence was considerable and Igino's wife and family were a little hostile to this new found relationship. It seemed to be taking up too much of his time and he seemed to be neglecting his political chances.

Chiara and the first meeting in the Dolomites

When Igino heard Chiara speak briefly at the meeting in the Montecitorio, he was sure that he had heard something new and immediately schemed to keep contact with her. In his typical style he writes in his sketch for an autobiography:

> I thought to myself, 'I mustn't lose touch with this person'. So I said to her, 'Why don't you write what you have just said to me to have it published in *Fides*?' I made her promise to do this and so I was able to keep in contact with her.*

* *Come conobbi i Focolari.* art. cit., p.44.

By several contacts with Chiara and with her focolare in Trent, he learnt to understand life anew and love. He saw people who loved one another as the children of God should. The overwhelming sense of love, which drives out all hatred, gradually weaned him away from politics. He began to apply the law of love to his whole life. It was for him a second conversion. Even his writing was changed:

> I saw that it was no longer a case of proving the existence of God to whoever denies it, but of showing in ourselves the life of God. *

As we have seen, he was a student of the Early Church and gradually he began to recognize that that was how it had been then. The pagan world was not converted by arguments, but by seeing how Christians loved one another. The young women in Trent impressed him by the way they went about their everyday life and yet, living in community, gave themselves totally to God. This was displayed in their love for one another and also in their love for the poor. But short visits to Trent were not enough.

In 1949, an opportunity presented itself. The focolare of Trent found it necessary to withdraw from the world during their vacation, and the obvious place for this was the holiday area which is the magnificent backdrop to Trent – the Dolomites. They withdrew to Tonadico. And Igino went with them. In that place, they gave life to what was later called the first 'Mariapolis' (City of Mary).

* ibid..

Champion of a little-known Movement

Igino Giordani did more than attend the meetings. He wrote about the Movement in his prestigious journal Fides. The article appeared in July 1950 and was based upon material Chiara had written for him:

The Focolares of Unity

Speaking of the 'Focolare Communities' that are beginning to multiply in France, Father Valliron writes in 'Temoignage Chrétien' that the Holy Spirit, who blows where he wills, today is evidentally blowing in this direction.

The French Movement is good, but very diverse and in my opinion less effective than that from Trent, which today is spreading like a fire throughout Italy, with the name, 'The Movement of Unity'. It is a name given just to have one, but in reality it concerns a Christian renaissance which assumes the aspect of a very lively conscience and above all of a very intense life in the Mystical Body by the members of this Movement. Their opponents have compared their universal aspirations and common ownership to the solidarity and communal form of Communism! But it is the Holy Spirit that conveys them, purifies them, until they become a free form of the Communion of Saints, translated into daily life, where Christians live together as brothers, and with God, as his children. They live together in unity with God and attain by his grace love which unites the brothers.

But let me tell a little of their history.

The story has been told already by a young woman from Trent in a style that echoes the simplicity of the Gospel. It carries the blessing of His Excellency, the Archbishop of Trent, Monsignor Carlo de Ferrari, who said: 'We confirm the substance of the above exposition, but also emphasise that the Movement, immediately it came to the notice of the diocesan authorities, gave motives for consolation which can be summed up thus: *the doing of excellent work, especially among young women; obedience in all things to their Ecclesiastical Superiors; no harm attributable to these persons, all faithful to the ideal: the Gospel lived in charity,* with the aim of reaching *unity* in Christ'.

Those last words sum up the ideal of the Movement. It was started in Trent during the bombing in 1944. Some young women, seeing buildings collapsing around them, and fortunes, illusions and riches, having learnt the vanity of all things, said in unison with the great mystics that God alone remains: *God alone.* And they understood the new commandment of the Gospel, that requires a limitless love of God and, through him, of one's neighbour. In what does love consist? In observing the commandments. From this first conviction, the communion of love lived from day to day with the Eucharist, they were pushed forward and meditated upon the sacred prayer of Jesus – his testimony – in which he prays that the love towards God and towards the neighbour will ultimately lead to making them one, by having perfect love and by giving to the world the witness of the divine origin of the message of Christ.

God manifests himself to the one who loves him, and also his neighbour, who is in the image of God and his creature. The neighbour is a creature of God, good or bad, rich or poor, male or female, to whom moment by moment the providence of God draws near. The Christian is made for love; he is a member of the race of God who is love.

And further, when two or three are gathered together in the name of Jesus, he is there among them; and in addition the presence of Jesus in the midst of them, in every moment and place, is enough to bring alive unity among them; the light comes on when you join the two poles of the electric current. And Christ is 'the true light that lightens every man coming into the world'.

Of such things the young women spoke in the air-raid shelters; and so they lived. And passing to practical things, they sold what they had and gave to the poor; and they lived in poverty together in a most modest apartment which they called a 'focolare'. The name suggests that a fire burns and spreads from that place: the fire of love. Every one of their company works in her own profession or trade. Meanwhile, in the focolare they begin to gather souls coming from every condition of society, who simply return to their own society, pledging themselves to live this charity to the point of reaching unity which the Lord left to us as his Testament. They create solidarity, spiritual communion, community; the kind of *koinonia*, which was reported in the Early Church in Jerusalem, when they were of one heart and soul, and they gave to others from their solidarity which spread from the supernatural plane to the human plane of economic help, so that there was not a needy person among them. *Therefore*, the Holy Spirit came upon them. These young women come together – usually every week – in a parish hall if the parish priest wishes it, or in a private house (it is recorded that the Early Church met in the house of Priscilla, of Aquila, of Caius) with the assistance only of a priest; and in a world preoccupied only with material things, they speak of spirituality; they seek the kingdom of God, convinced that God will give them what is lacking; and this proves to be their experience. In the focolares and in the Communities, the words of the Gospel are seen to come alive, 'Give and it shall be given to you'; that proves to be true every day among them.

I say focolares: since, as the number of young women grows, they seek out other lodgings in Trent; other focolares are formed; and they spread beyond the region of Trent. Now in Rome there are flourishing focolares both for men and for women. The spirit of the Focolare – to love God and for him to make themselves one with their brother, so that the brother becomes an access to God, and thus to live in constant union with the Lord – this spirit penetrates into monastic houses, into the circles of Catholic Action, into private families, into institutions of various kinds and – incredible as it may seem – into the Italian Parliament! And everywhere it revives the conscience, recovers hope, sustains joy, restores a meaning to life, experienced moment by moment as total abandonment to the will of God, in which, as Dante knew, 'is our peace'. Radical conversions take place. The Gospel reappears in all its original freshness; the Church lives in all its virginal maternity. From the boredom of a life characterized by anxiety and fear, the liberty of the children of God is set free, with the joy of experiencing unity with him.

The focolares and the communities, which live under ecclesiastical discipline, do not wish to supplant any other institution or Movement; they carry a flame and a light, which adds to all others, but does not replace them. The members are left to their own vocations and conditions; they do not receive a membership card nor a badge, do not pay a subscription, are not bound by any rules, beyond those of the Church; they therefore conserve full liberty; as it is with this ideal, inspired by the Paraclete, as with the wind which you know not whence it comes or whither it goes.

In the liberty of the children of God, whoever embraces this Ideal, which is the Gospel, is renewed in spirit; becoming the new man, of which St. Paul speaks. A Christian without qualification: total.

And this renewal, this second conversion, is the fruit of a process of collective sanctification. It is, in a way, socialized, in which each is sanctified with the other and for the other. The process is facilitated by a simplified vision of the word of life (the Gospel) meditated daily with the Church, from which the interior perfection is brought within the reach of every soul. Jesus has in fact asked that all – and there is no *elite* in this – should be perfect as our Father in heaven is perfect, while he communicates to tractable spirits, via sanctifying grace, the very life of God. The great mystical truth is drawn from riches, old and new, from the casket of the religious orders and placed at the disposal of the laity; there is democratization – in homes, in garages, on the streets, so that one is always with God and with one's brother. In this way, at a time of the most tremendous testing of the faith, the barriers that by chance have been erected between the contemplative life and the active life, between the religious community and the great mass of the laity, are broken down in a certain series, so that by freely and easily circulating the resources of the Holy Spirit, religious and laity rally together against atheism.

There are no records kept, but by this time in Italy, France, Germany, China, Mexico, the United States, there are innumerable souls who have found peace and joy in living this ideal, in which there is nothing new and everything new (like the Gospel itself, which is always the same and always rich in surprises and resources), carried primarily by simple young women, because it pleases God to confound the wise and to honour the humble, as our technological society regards them, and perhaps because in a society where the woman often exercises a charm of degradation, it was suitable that women should initiate a work of purification by which it may be possible to say that Mary passes along the streets of Italy. She passes and opens, delicately and with strength, the doors to Christ the King.*

The crucial 10 years

From 1949 to 1959, Mariapolises were held in Tonadico, Siror, Fiera di Primiero, and Val di Fassa. These beautiful villages of the Dolomites became legendary names in the Focolare Movement and featured in their earliest songs. Igino Giordani was in at the beginning. It was in Tonadico that he was given what he then called his word of life. These meetings of the Movement began quite small, as we have seen, but they grew over the years. They became important occasions for deepening the life of the Movement and for the growth in number of those involved. Away from the usual strains of daily life, focolarini could share testimonies and put Jesus in the midst, and experience the true sense of unity.

Later, there would be permanent Mariapolises as well

* Art. in 'Fides', July, 1950, pp. 206-208.

as shorter gatherings in many countries, but in these early days, they were holiday periods and richly enjoyed. Igino was spiritually enriched by what he experienced there and in particular he seems, according to his diary, to have grasped the essence of the Movement as love – true love which shines out, not in words alone, but in deeds.

Some years later, in an interview in which he spoke about the effect of his joining the Movement upon many other politicians (including the Prime Minister, Alcide De Gasperi), Igino Giordani caught the atmosphere of those early Mariapolises. His presence in the Focolare proved that if a Member of Parliament could be converted, anyone could be converted. In the same interview, he said:

> It created a breach in a long-standing social attitude and prejudice that was saturated with laicism and anticlericalism. The charity that had come from the Focolare recreated the spiritual bond between laity and priesthood and, as a consequence, between the profane and the sacred, the world and the Church, marriage and virginity. It helped rebuild a community where all differences vanished in the fire of charity.*

This discovery of the role of the laity in the Church, which he had sought all his life, was the great discovery. The Focolare offered him holiness and he saw that he was not shunned from that world by his married state or his involvement in politics. He did not cease to extol the virtue of virginity, but he saw also the holiness of marriage; he did not deny the sacred vocation of the religious, but he saw a duty to be holy also in the world. This grew as he continued in contact with Chiara and as he met the growing community of the Focolare. In fact, his joining encouraged growth – from unlikely quarters. He continues in that interview:

* Lorit and Grimaldi, op. cit., p.57f..

Once the news spread, quite a few members of the Italian Parliament joined in, among whom were Pacati, Roselli, and Foresi, whose son was to become a priest in the Focolare and, later on, the ecclesiastical assistant of the Movement. Once, even Premier De Gasperi came to see us, having met us by chance in Fregene in 1949. He said that he was sorry he could not stay for dinner because of urgent state affairs (shortages of bread, threats of upheaval in Italy). Nevertheless, after coming to visit us for what he said would be a brief visit, the conversation went on until late at night. As he said goodbye that night, he told me: 'This morning I woke up with a sense of despair, but you have given me hope once more.'*

That was fairly typical of those early Mariapolises. Carelessness of time, unexpected visitors, despair turned to hope, as Jesus is put in the midst. Some of those members of the Italian Parliament were present when Giordani made his famous speech against War and the joining of NATO. They were few, but they understood and encouraged him as he sat down.

The last of the Mariapolises in the Dolomites

We are fortunate to have an account of the Mariapolis held in the Dolomites in 1959, written by a visitor from England, an authority on prayer, Olive Wyon, who had a great genius for recognizing the genuine in spiritual movements. Frequently she urged me to go to the Dolomites and involve myself in this experience as Igino Giordani had done. Her account is given briefly in a little book called 'Living Streams', now out of print:

At a recent rally in the Dolomites there were 12,000 people present representing 20 nations and speaking 9 languages. . . , a revival based on the Word of Life, in the

* ibid. p.58.

heart of the Catholic Church in Italy. This revival is still going on and is spreading into other countries even as far away as Latin America. There is nothing 'separatist' or 'sectarian' about this movement. Its members are loyal Catholics, living 'in the world'. They lay great stress on love in action, in daily life, as well as in social relationships. It is not easy to describe this movement because it is always on the move. It seems to grow by a sort of cheerful and hopeful infection from one small group to another, all of them determined as far as they can, to do the will of God to the utmost, to *live* the Gospel before they preach it. As their name suggests, this movement is a fire, which is spreading by leaps and bounds. *

That lively description by Olive Wyon who knew the Movement only by her visit, but who had the spiritual sensitivity to discern the power of the Focolare 'fire', shows why Igino Giordani found it infectious. He could not leave it. And once he joined, his urge to go out to others became more powerful than ever. It is right to call him a co-founder of the Movement with Chiara.

The politics of love

The memorable speech made by Igino Giordani in the Italian Parliament on 16th March 1949 was the expression of a spiritual attitude that inspired his political position that was sharply pacifistic and antimilitary. It marked him as a controversial figure. Alcide De Gasperi saw no political future for one who could argue against NATO and urge Italy to present herself as neutral and pacifist. At that time, 'peace' was a political word. When Eisenhower visited Italy in 1951, Giordani was courted by the left and reviled by the right. He saw the West and the East as representing the

* Olive Wyon, 'Living Streams', SCM Press, 1963, p.119.

'politics of power (or war)'. He substituted the 'politics of love'. In the Focolare's instinctive sense of the power of love he saw a sound philosophical and religious base. He discovered that in personal and social relationships the greatest power in the world is love. He saw this acted out among the young people of the Focolare and he helped them to understand what they were doing.

The influence of St. Catherine of Siena was considerable, but his true source, like hers, was in Mary. *L'Opera di Maria* attracted him as much as 'fire' in the Focolare. He saw that Mary had given Christ to the world in love. He went back to that.

He was, of course, a devout Catholic, and the devotion of Chiara to the Church was one of her attractions; but he knew the weaknesses of the Church structures better than she did. These weaknesses did not turn him against the Church. It was in the Church that he found Mary. There are two entries in his diary which illustrate this clearly:

[1957:] 18 February – A person converted to God from a life of sin, after several years of life in a convent, confessed to me her disappointment and her intention to pass on to other experiences, in order to find Christ. I told her that Christ's will is unity: 'That all may be one': and that to separate oneself is equivalent to setting oneself against his Will. She complained of the avarice she had encountered, the rigidity of the written law: and I told her that before God we are not responsible for the ill deeds of others: we are responsible for what we do, each of us, to obey the divine law. The failings of others do not exonerate me from giving love. Christ lives and the Church is holy provided I let him live in me and I become holy. Evils are not eliminated by flying from them but by opposing good to them, making of our persons a barrier of virtue; and the ills of the Church's body are not cured by adding a further ill; that would be a desertion.*

* 'Diary of Fire', op. cit., p.51.

We can detect in that entry some of the personal conversations he had at the Mariapolises in the Dolomites. He is talking about more than personal piety and is certainly opposed to separation. His advice to oppose good to evil was in practice also in politics. The practice of the Focolare was both influencing him and he was helping them.

The second quote shows more clearly the source of his 'politics of love' in Mary: this concerns a deeply religious experience he had on 1st October 1957 – a month sacred to the Virgin Mary. He recounts that experience in the entry in his diary for *6th October*:

> . . . after prayers, all of a sudden my soul was cleared of human things and persons and in their place, Mary entered, together with Jesus, drained of his Blood, and the whole abode of my soul was filled by her figure of suffering and of love. And with her in me I grasped the frivolity of my attachment to transient things. For twenty-four hours, she was there, like an altar holding the victim: *Virgo altare Christi*, the Virgin, Christ's altar. My soul was her abode, her temple. But at the end of twenty four hours, sharing in her anguish and love for her brought about a unity between her and my soul and it seemed that she became my soul: she was no longer my guest, but I was her guest, so that I could say: 'It is no longer I who live but Mary who lives in me'.*

From that mystical experience came the decision to change the attitude of his former life – 'Her presence had . . . virginized my soul', he wrote. He no longer needed to look at shrines or images of the Virgin. He had only to turn his eyes within. All that month of October, he trembled at the thought of this experience. But the decisions affecting his outer life, springing directly from this experience were made in the next few weeks and are recorded:

* ibid. p.53.

15 November – I feel that I have arrived at the autumn of life: the last fruits have been gathered and eaten, the last leaves have been blown away by cold gusts of wind. I am well aware of it: my inward youthfulness resists, as if fortified by trials: this lack of affections and satisfactions coming from men have tempered it, sharpened it as it were, made it a prow that advances towards the Mystery: so that the plant seems to gather itself together to bear fruit again in eternity.

I have endeavoured for decades, without growing discouraged and ever starting afresh at the beginning, to give myself to persons and to institutions, to ideals and to services; and it seemed to me that I was giving myself as though consecrating myself without counting the cost, joyfully. Now, it seems, as I look back on it, that I sowed failures to reap a harvest of ingratitude, as if persons and things, one after the other, had exploited and deceived me. They have all taken, few or none have given. *

The astonishing thing is that this was written in 1957 when Igino Giordani could have had all he wanted of political power or success. This is not an old man regretting the things he was never given, but a man in the midst of life, recognizing true values. He is disappointed with politics, but not because he has failed. He is disappointed with the fallen values of political life and in his new spiritual quest he is sad that he has given so much to this worthless period. In it, he has known the Spring and the full Summer. Now he sees all its fruits falling in the Autumn. It is the autumn of his political life – not the autumn of his life, for that is just beginning:

The fruit and the leaves fall but from their decayed substance flowers a new Spring. In the solitude which is taking over in preparation for winter God stands out: he is drawing near; and my relationship with him is becoming more intimate and more immediate. To the extent that it loses in the human economy, it is gaining in

* ibid. p.54f..

the divine economy. Creatures detach themselves in order that I may become attached to the Creator. I fail to find love, in order that I may find Love.*

In this period of his diary, Igino Giordani is rich in phrases which catch the mood of his conversion state: 'In God there is no more history', 'Life is only a process of ripening', 'God who transplants the tree into paradise gathers the fruit', 'God has accepted the homage of my writings and takes them at their word. Now he wishes that after having penned them I should live them'. Then comes the sad and yet triumphant entry of *26th February 1958*:

> The pruning continues. Friendships, hopes, joys, have been cut away. As a writer, I am not read; as a Catholic, I am not welcomed; as a politician, I am disregarded. I had bound myself to a religious family and found joy in communion in Christ and in a common life in Mary. My dilettantism and my pretensions, my judgement and my inability to obey have made the connection impossible for me and in any case it was of itself almost severed; maintained only by slender threads. I would be inclined to level reproaches of inconsistency and ingratitude, but who will assure me that they would not arise from wounded self-love and would not damage charity? Better to retreat into silence . . . I would like to cry out: My God, my God, why have you forsaken me? – but I am afraid of mouthing rhetoric.†

But he does not continue in that desolate mood. He writes of the

> inflow, of a fine and serene joy, as if from a deep peace; and it is like the perfume of lilies and roses, flowering in a sunken garden, and its name is Mary.‡

---

* ibid. p.55.
† ibid. p.57.
‡ ibid. . . .

184

Marriage and the Church

A major problem for any spiritual movement in the Catholic Church, before the Second Vatican Council, was the traditional tendency to confine purity to a celibate priesthood and the cult of virginity among consecrated women. For Igino this had been a life-long problem. He was the father of a happy family. His married state imposed a strain upon his longing for complete commitment to God. His church always saw such a commitment in terms of celibacy. This led him, as he often says, to feel a second class citizen in the Church. It seemed that only the priests and the virgins could keep company with the angels. But his life in the world of politics led him equally to reject its sub-Christian values. He knew that he must sooner or later withdraw from that world. But any movement in the direction of spiritual commitment was blocked by the fact that, while the Church made good use of him, it never regarded him as fit for holiness. The Focolare gave him a wholly new view of the Church. As he watched these communities of mostly young people, living in total commitment to the 'Ideal', he saw the Church being lived in the world. They did not regard him as a second class citizen in the kingdom of heaven; they welcomed him as one of themselves. He helped them to express this by the admission of married focolarini into membership of the Movement; and they later became the animators of the 'New Families'.

As we shall see later, the 'New Families Movement' became one of the most effective parts of the Movement, recognized as such by Pope John Paul II. But we are at present dealing with a much earlier period, even before the Second Vatican Council of Pope John XXIII. He found himself with virgins, priests and the whole of the

185

Church. Their treasures, their contemplation of virtues became his. Rapidly this became his whole life. Again it was to St. Catherine that he returned – to a familiar passage – and recalled that she had said that you have to build yourself a cell, spiritually, and contemplate God within it. This he did, and there is ample evidence in his diary, that it was within his family life.

A human divine triangle

Later, when Igino Giordani was more often called 'Foco' within the family of the Focolare, he worked out these ideas on marriage and Church in diagrammatic form. 'The priesthood, virginity and marriage are the three sides of an isosceles triangle'. The traditional virtues of the Church, illustrated by the celibate priesthood and virginity, are the upright sides. The base on the earth is marriage. Marriage extends itself across the earth, 'giving birth to priests and virgins, through whom it communicates with heaven'. That still seems to give marriage an inferior place with the purpose only of producing children who might aspire to virtue! But Foco learnt to go further. Both the celibate priesthood and virginity may 'carry graces from God', but marriage 'incarnates them; and reciprocally gathers from humanity the requests that, by means of those two, it raises to heaven'.*

* cf. ibid. p.63.; this quotataion retranslated from the Italian: *'Diario di fuoco'*, Città Nuova, Rome, 1980, p.83.

3

The International Dimension

The climax of the Mariapolises in the Dolomites came in 1959, at Fiera di Primiero, when a vast crowd of more than ten thousand people were assembled and plans were made for future 'cities' of this kind. In 1960, the Mariapolis was held in Fribourg, Switzerland, and after that they began to spread all over the world. Even though there was already the idea of a permanent Mariapolis, this was not possible at that time. It was some years later that, apart from the temporary Mariapolises, permanent centres of witness to the Gospel were established: in Loppiano (Italy), Fontem (West Cameroon), O'Higgins (Argentina) and other places.

Already in the last Mariapolis held at Fiera di Primiero in 1959, a strongly international dimension was evident, when there were twenty seven different nations represented. This international dimension is a common characteristic of both the Mariapolises and many other meetings of the Movement, and Giordani fitted quite naturally into it, for he had had worldwide contacts even before he met Chiara.

The international contacts

A poor boy in Tivoli at the beginning of this century had
no opportunity or hope of international travel. But the
young Igino glimpsed another world when he made
friends with a Rumanian family in Tivoli and worked on
the Rumanian language to see how much it corresponded
to the tiburtina dialect of Tivoli.

His early work with the *Partito Popolare Italiano* brought
him into contact with international issues and his discussions with Don Sturzo must have widened his view. His
writing at that time required the reading of notices and
news from many different lands. When Don Sturzo had to
leave him, his last piece of advice was, 'Learn English'.

Igino Giordani's first travel abroad, however, was to
the USA to learn how to catalogue a library. He kept his
eyes open and followed up contacts. He also met the
Protestant Churches in force.

During his period in the Vatican Library, he read more
than the Church Fathers. He encouraged all with whom
he had come in contact in the USA, France and England
(both of which he visited en route) to send journals and
newspapers. As he edited 'Fides', he made good use of
those foreign periodicals as he kept the Italian clergy in
contact with what was happening outside Italy. A new
Methodist church opened in Harpenden, Herts., England,
is described in one issue, outlining its special arrangements
for children's work. The progress of the Ecumenical
Movement is documented, sometimes critically, but
always informatively.

When the war ended, 'Fides' showed an even greater
interest in other countries and in the Ecumenical Movement. There is a report of the First Assembly of the
World Council of Churches in 1948, which shows
considerable knowledge of the problems involved.

1950 was the Holy Year and all the world came to Rome. Igino Giordani's close association with the recently appointed Pope Pius XII meant that he was much involved in meeting visitors from other countries. His linguistic abilities were useful, because he could speak both English and German reasonably well, in addition to French and of course Italian. He was known as a cultured man, a distinguished writer and many took the opportunity to see him and talk with him about the ways in which their countries had fared during the war. The list is too long to repeat, but they included Daniel-Rops who wrote an introduction to the French translation of Giordani's best known book to date – 'The Sign of Contradiction'. There were many who had read Giordani's work on the social teaching of the Churches, either in Italian or in translation. Americans sought him out also.

As Deputy in the Italian Parliament he had been involved in international discussions and when he took a stand against the membership of Italy in NATO, his speech against war was widely circulated. This attitude and the distinguished defence of it in the speech, which was subsequently published, led to invitations to many parts of Europe. In the fifties, Igino Giordani already had an international reputation in political affairs. In 1959, from 21st October to 8th December, he made a memorable visit to Asia with his son, Brando. He was still full of his own spiritual development and his newly found inspiration in the Focolare Movement. Igino enjoyed the journey and brought his impressions of the needs of the Third World to the Focolare Movement.

In 1945, during the liturgy for the feast of Christ the King Chiara had been very struck by the words of the psalm: 'Ask, and I will give you all the peoples of the world', but she did not know what to do with it. She treasured it. The meeting with Igino Giordani helped her to see what it meant and all kinds of contacts became possible. Later, Chiara would travel to a considerable extent, seeking unity with the Orthodox Church in Constantinople, with the Lutherans in Germany and with the Anglicans in Canterbury. She has even travelled to Asia and, particularly in Japan, sought unity with the other religions, such as Buddhism.

But in the early years, when the contact with other Christian denominations and with other religions had not yet begun, Chiara's meeting with Igino Giordani must certainly have been a help for her to glimpse future developments, such as the universal, ecumenical dimension of the Movement, and its expansion over the whole world which she had foreseen at that Mass on the feast of Christ the King.

The secret of growth

The brief comment on the Mariapolises in the Dolomites may have disguised the phenomenal growth of the Movement. Look again at those early Mariapolises as Giordani counted them in an interview several years ago:

> The first year there were seven persons; the second year there were two hundred; the third four thousand, and by the fourth year it had become a problem to accommodate everybody!*

When he was asked by a parish priest from Trent in 1951, 'What did you do to grow in such incredible proportions and with such speed?' Giordani replied with a twinkle in his eye, 'Well, we did some advertising'. The priest laughed because he knew there had been no advertising. In fact, the Focolare Movement has been

* Lorit and Grimaldi, op. cit., p.60.

extraordinarily slow in using the mass media, although when they did, they did it superbly well. At first, Giordani had been anxious to write some articles, but he was advised to stop by Bishop De Ferrari. This was, of course after the 'Fides' article of 1950.

It had been the same with ecumenical relations. Almost unnoticed, the Focolare entered into fraternal relations with Anglicans, Greek Orthodox, Baptists, Episcopalians and even with Buddhists and Muslims. It had become a social and religious apostolate, from politics to ecumenism, from family to youth. And in all this, Igino Giordani used his rich experience. He saw the effects of the Movement in homes and workshops, in restaurants and at trades union meetings. This expansion has found structure in a series of movements which support and regulate the growth – the New Humanity Movement, the New Families Movement, the Parishes Movement – which by their very names indicate an updating and renewing of social structures and activities.

Giordani soon discovered that he was accomplishing far more, even at the social and political level through the Focolare Movement, than he would ever have achieved through the Italian Parliament. And he did not have to compromise his 'Ideal'.

The visit to Asia

In 1959, Igino Giordani made his first and only visit to Asia. It was the result of two pressures and like almost everything he did, it was pioneering work. A Catholic Order of missionary nuns (the Canossian Sisters) had been very kind to Don Sturzo when he was in danger and exile and when, after the war, he returned to Italy.

Igino wanted to do something for them and when he

asked, they suggested that he write a book about their work. As this was principally in Asia, that would mean a tour of their Asian stations. At the same time, Brando – Ildebrando to give him his full name – was developing into an experienced film producer and was flexing his muscles in TV. So much has happened in TV since 1959, that it is difficult to remember what a startling proposal it was to go to Asia to make a TV programme! TV was still in its infancy in Europe. There were no satellites and the range of most European programmes was confined to Europe. It had been revolutionary enough to form a European Broadcasting Union and then to develop what later became virtually a European network through Eurovision. This was pretty well the extent of most TV producers' vision. The complicated plans which meant offering a programme to the E.B.U. and decisions by each company whether that country could take it, the technical difficulties if one company did not want it, all this occupied our minds as national companies gradually widened their horizons. Films, of course, were used extensively in TV. But it was usual for the film to be made for quite other distribution, through cinemas etc., and then if it looked promising to use it some time later for TV. Outside TV coverage was usually confined to the country concerned or offered by some other European company. In those days, TV producers did not travel as they do today!

Brando saw the possibilities early and when his father had a request to write a book that required a visit to Asia and probably some visuals, he proposed to the Italian TV that he should go to Asia searching for film material for TV. Similiar travel had been done for several years in Radio and Brando was among those pioneers who attempted it for TV. The television programme on the missions of the Canossian Sisters in the East, with

192

Igino's comment, had a great success in Italy and it won the various prizes, including The International UNDA prize.

The crew

Compared with the battalion of operators who today travel for the production of TV programmes to any part of the world, the little crew that left Italy for Asia seems very small indeed. Brando had one camera man. These two operators were accompanied by Brando's wife, Silvia, and his father. There are few notes in the diary about this Asian visit, but we can be sure that the new scenes and the new adventures quickened Igino's imagination.

He had not been travelling abroad for several years. This time he was starting for Asia with a youthful enthusiasm: 'We are going to see where the Church is being born!' he used to tell his friends, thus announcing the trip with the small television group. Whenever he travelled he found inspiration from the newness of his surroundings and he observed with utmost care the characteristics of the people he met. As a young man in the USA he had done that and recorded his impressions in his 'English' diary. He did not hesitate to pass judgement either in these notes. Igino was a born journalist and an imaginative writer. When in 1948, he and Mya went to the Moral Rearmament hotel at Caux, above Montreux in Switzerland, he was at once moved by the scenery and sympathetic to the people. The diary again contains little mention of this visit, but an article he wrote for 'Il Popolo' and later translated for 'New World News' shows the excitement that new scenes and new places aroused in him:

As you arrive at Caux-sur-Montreux, 3,000 feet above sea level, you are filled with wonder. You seem to be in Dreamland. It is not only the long range of the Savoy Alps bordering on the lake of Geneva, and the shining glaciers of the Dents du Midi that take your breath away. It is the whole life of the place which captures your heart, the life which is lived against that background of green and silver, in the corridors and gardens of the great hotel which has become the home and headquarters of Moral Rearmament in Europe.*

Then, he had been struck by the fact that:

Indians and Chinese, Burmese and Scandinavians, Italians and Austrians, Americans and coloured folk, speaking all languages, princes of royal blood and workers with calloused hands, men and women, young and old, all lived simply together on a level of equality.†

He would not find that 'level of equality' in Asia, but he soon discovered the teeming millions of people of all kinds. Some of his impressions he stored up and poured into the book he had come to write. It was published in the following year, *'Ho visto la Chiesa nascente'* ('I Have Seen the Church Being Born'). The book was published by Città Nuova, the publishing firm of the Focolare Movement in Rome, 1960. It was illustrated with some of the photographs Brando or his camera had taken, some of them in colour. Although it is the account of the missionary work which he visited, it is also a good assessment of the impact of Asia upon Igino Giordani's mind and imagination at that time.

* Art. in 'New World News' (The Journal of the Moral Rearmament Movement), 1948.
† ibid..

India

The country which impressed him most was clearly India, not so much Bombay, but the rich fields of Kerala. When they welcomed him at one mission station, the nuns had taught the girls to sing in Italian, a popular Italian song to welcome their distinguished visitors. Igino was amused to hear a thoroughly 'fascist' song, because the nuns had last known Italy under Fascism. His amusement contrasts strongly with his earlier reactions to every remembrance of the regime he hated! The gathering years and the Focolare Movement had taught him tolerance and understanding. He did not stop to correct their political tendencies, but accepted the welcome they had so carefully prepared, with warmth and grace.

Most of the cheerful photographs which Silvia and Brando showed me were of a family group and there is no doubt that Igino Giordani was in his element. Something of the spirit of his own earlier book about his children which was constantly rewritten, *'La repubblica dei marmocchi'*, emerges in the stories told of that trip around India. The fun of a house full of children, which never allowed him to take himself too seriously, came back during those days and weeks together.

There were other countries after India and the colour of Asia, its wisdom and meditation, impressed him, but so did its poverty. The various types of people he met, Chinese, Singhalese, Filipinos and the Japanese, each taught something of the richness of humanity.

He kept close to his original brief of writing a book about the missionary work of the nuns, but he learnt far more than what they had to show him. By the time he reached Japan, he was perhaps tired and anxious to get back to his work in Italy. He never did like long periods away, and moreover, Japan did not stir him as India had done.

He returned weary but contented. And I am sure he had much to tell Chiara. He had seen at first hand how much the Church was appreciated in those lands, seen its vitality, its capacity to answer the many questions of those peoples. His sensitivity to the aim of the Movement to contribute to the unity of all in Christ, fulfilling Jesus' prayer 'that all may be one', made him glimpse future possibilities for the missionary endeavour and for dialogue with the ancient religions of the orient. The presence of the Movement, through several missionaries in Asia, will also have been a reason for hope for him.

What 'Foco' said about the Movement in Asia, in 1959, we do not know. It is impossible to believe, however, that he did not speak much of a new experience that had so changed his life. And yet he was always discrete in what he said. After his death I talked with Brando and Sergio, the two younger sons, and they both said that they had learnt more about the Focolare Movement after his death than they had ever known while he was alive. 'He never forced anything on us', Sergio said. Then, once he was back in Italy, he took up his work in the heart of the Movement again.

The ecumenical activities

The first activities of this kind were not planned. Individuals and, later, groups met spontaneously until 1960. At that time, due to the increasing number of contacts, more structured activities became necessary. The structures grew slowly, first with Lutherans in Germany, which led to a joint centre of Lutheran and Catholic at Ottmaring in Bavaria (1965); then with

Anglicans, which led to an annual conference in Rome immediately after Easter (1965). Later activities were organized in North America, with its bewildering variety of denominations, Australia and the Middle East. Igino Giordani was in the midst of all this activity. In 1967, relations were opened with Eastern Christianity. Chiara was invited by Patriarch Athenagoras to go to Istanbul. His great soul was consumed with the desire for unity. He wanted to know Chiara because he had guessed her importance in the field of unity, and he wanted to find out from her all about the Focolare Movement. What she said to the Patriarch in that meeting was by now also the spiritual heritage of Giordani, the committed builder of unity who had turned from polemics to being more concerned to respect and to love. He was completely with Chiara in this. She said: 'For many years we believed that the spirituality of the Movement was only for Catholics; but because of the strong stress that is placed on the life of the Scriptures, we later realized that it was for all Christians who live it in accordance with their beliefs and with what the Holy Spirit suggests to them'.*

Igino Giordani's growth in ecumenical attitudes, learnt from Chiara, is documented by himself: 'The conversion (i.e. after his acceptance of and by the Focolare) which was accomplished in me was evident in my style as a polemical writer: from that time on, I tried rather to convince [*convincere*] than to conquer [*vincere*]'.

Ugo Piazza had compared him in debate to a stainless steel hammer, but now he appeared more like someone simply clothed in a mantle. (The pun is on *martello* (hammer) and *mantello* (cloak).) 'The keen intellect which drove home his sharp polemic', Ugo Piazza wrote, 'is

---

* Lorit and Grimaldi, op. cit., p.139.

enlarged now to include love in the truth and to speak the truth in mutual love'.

In 1961, after some German pastors had heard Chiara speak and expressed their surprise at the idea of Catholics 'living the Gospel' and wished to disseminate information about the spirituality of the Focolare Movement, a centre was opened in Rome for ecumenical affairs. This was called, appropriately, 'Centro Uno'. It was obvious that Igino Giordani was the most suitable person in the Movement to direct it and this he did from the start. Centro Uno was to be a place of meeting and reference for the ecumenical work of the Focolare Movement. In its office, which was situated in Piazza di Tor Sanguigna, close to the famous Piazza Navona in Rome, Igino Giordani worked daily for 15 years and then for another 6 years, though in a more restful fashion.

Pope John XXIII and the Second Vatican Council

Chiara was always fully part of her Church and ready to act upon its least desires, so she found herself in profound harmony with it in ecumenical affairs. This was true of her approach as the maturing of time brought about new attitudes to ecumenism. So many encyclicals had warned against any compromise – 'Satis Cognitum' (1896) of Leo XIII, 'Mortalium Animos' (1948) of Pius XI, 'Mystici Corporis' (1943) of Pius XII, 'Monitum cum Compertum' (1948) and even the Instructio, 'Ecclesia Catholica' (1950). All these documents seemed to imply that the only ecumenism that the Roman Catholic Church could entertain was 'submission'. Then Pope John XXIII began to speak. He seemed to reverse the trend of the Instructio of 1950, which had forbidden certain attitudes because of the danger of indifferentism. Vittorio Subilia lists these in his book, 'The Problem of Catholicism': 'To add the truths held by non-Catholics to those formulated in Catholic dogma, "silently" to overlook controversial points of view, to concentrate on the things which unite, and to keep quiet on those which divide, utterances, that is, in which anti- or pre-ecumenical formula of "Return" *seems* to be replaced by "Encounter".'* It is difficult to avoid the conclusion that there has been a radical change of attitude.

Pope John acted in love rather than logic and he certainly gave the impression of radical change which was borne out by the subsequent effect of the Second Vatican Council. The Pope explained that the Council was to be first and foremost a domestic matter for the Catholic Church, essentially designed 'to bring again to the face of the Church of Jesus Christ, that splendour which was etched there at its birth and in its simplest and purest lines, and to render it once more what its Divine Founder made it . . . a time to gather about the Church in a study of love, to rediscover the characteristics of her age of youth and vigour, and to set them together once more' (13th November 1960).†

For such a change, Igino Giordani had been prepared by Chiara. His own knowledge of the Early Church was matched to the hour and the emphasis on love which he had learnt afresh from Chiara, enabled him to catch the spirit of this unusual Pope and to champion him. For it seemed as though Pope John were redecorating the house of the Church to receive its separated children back. The Catholic Church was prepared to change. And it was prepared to change along the lines urged by the best of the reformers since John Wycliffe.

---

* Vittorio Subilia, 'The Problem of Catholicism' (English edition of *'Il problema del cattolicesimo'*), Claudiania, Turin, 1962, p.14.
† cf. *'Encicliche e discorsi di Giovanni XXIII'*, Vol. II, Rome, 1963, p.322

The Second Vatican Council stirred up the brightest of its children in support and protest, but it moved forward. In all this, the Focolare Movement kept close to the hierarchy. And, under Chiara's guidance, the Movement followed all its directives which brought to ecumenism that richness of views and those fruits which are proper to genuine Christianity. Centro Uno, directed by Giordani, was a useful instrument in the Movement's contribution to the opening of the Catholic Church to dialogue with other Churches. Igino Giordani had already shown his understanding of the need for reform along the lines of return to the Early Church and in this connection he had linked it with the social concern of the Church for the poor. His most widely read books were those about the social teaching of Jesus, the New Testament Church and the Early Church. He also developed an understanding of the Eucharist in its relation to the Agape as the means of forming Communion. 'Therefore,' he says at the conclusion of his address during the Ecumenical Week in April 1972, 'the sacrifice of the Mass is made up of two parts: one that is Christ's and the other that is the poor man's, the poor man who is a 'poor man of Christ', in the sense that Christ can be seen and served in him'.

He cannot resist a quotation from Tertullian, his old master, which allows him a moment for his old rhetoric: 'The name of these meals [Agape – love] . . . defines their purpose. Through them we look after the poor not in the way you pagans feed your parasites, selling them food at the price of countless insults, but by looking after them as people worthy of every respect and honour, whose humble condition makes them even more commendable to the eyes of the Eternal One'.*

Gabriella Fallacara, who has taken over Giordani's

* Art. in 'New City', June 1972.

work at Centro Uno recalls those 15 years of his work, many of which she shared with him, in an article for 'Città Nuova', published later in the same year by 'Unitas'. She writes that 'he brought the richness of his views, rendered simple by his style of humour, the wisdom of his interpretation of events, the brightness of a worker who knew how to hope and to wait, but who never put off until tomorrow what he could do today.'*

The years that followed

From 1961 until his death in 1980, Giordani participated in 35 ecumenical conferences, run by the Movement through Centro Uno. This meant considerable organization. Beside participating in the public affairs of these conferences, he had valuable private conversations with representatives of Churches of all kinds from Europe, the Middle East and the United States. During this period he also continued to write for many newspapers, magazines, journals and 'Città Nuova', the Movement's magazine in Italian. These periodicals provided a platform from which he sought to sensitize the 'collective memory' to the duty of Christian unity by reporting conferences and discussions, as well as actual unions of Churches, from the whole range of the ecumenical world. When Cardinal Bea died (1968), he paid tribute to him as an enlightened champion and pioneer of unity who had battled and lived for it:

> During the years of the Council and in those that followed, there was not to be found among the Christians of all the Churches, a person who longed for unity more than Cardinal Bea. Because he was able to interpret

---

* *Pioniere dell' ecumenismo,* art. in 'Città Nuova', no.9, 1980.

the greatest aspirations of contemporary ecumenism and present and defend them with a prudence coupled with a remarkable daring, he was revered by people of every class, race and faith throughout the world . . . It was Cardinal Bea who gave to our Movement the Holy Spirit as its patron. He was impressed by the programmes of the Focolare, based on the ideal of unity which is the apex of charity, to be brought into a world threatened by divisive ideologies and political hegemony, and pushed by technology into becoming a desert of individualism, disparate and isolated.*

When he moved into the focolare at Rocca di Papa in May 1974, he was already getting old in years, although in the Focolare, as he said, 'It is forbidden to grow old', he could no longer go to Centro Uno every day. The distance was too great for that. But he went twice a week and the rest of his work he carried on from the Mariapolis Centre. It was in fact at Rocca di Papa that many of the Christians of various countries got to know him.

Again it is Gabriella Fallacara who gives us a vivid picture of Giordani:

I remember him as direct and youthful, with the heart of a patriarch, spontaneous in humility and steady in prayer. He possessed a tremendous capacity for communication with young people, important personalities, and with ecumenists, whether they be bishops of the Orthodox Church, the Reformed Church, the Anglican Communion, or followers of Zwingli and Calvin. People of the most varied backgrounds found themselves taken up in a dialogue that often 'opened new horizons'.†

---

* cf. ibid., p.50.
† ibid..

Pope Paul VI

Igino Giordani had been the friend of Popes before. Perhaps his closest relationship was with Pope Pius XII, who encouraged and supported his work in the Vatican Library and whose Biography he eventually wrote. The opening of Centro Uno in 1960 brought him into close contact with Pope John XXIII and he played his part in the Second Vatican Council. A few months after that Council began, Pope John was dead and it fell to the new Pope Paul VI to carry through to the end and carry the responsibility for putting many of its decisions into practice. Pope Paul had shown favour to the Movement ever since he had been Substitute for the Secretary of State. From 1965 to 1978, the Pope greeted sections of the Movement in St. Peter's, showing always a personal interest in what they were doing. One Sunday in the Holy Year, 1975, Pope Paul was moved at the sight of the great crowd of young people from every country who filled the square. The spirit of his greeting then was typical:

> We have seen this morning, around the altar, together with other pilgrims, 20,000 believers, mostly young, who call themselves *Gen* – 'new generation' – come together from all over the world. A beautiful Movement. We thank God and take courage. A new world is born, a Christian world of faith and love. I call upon Mary for you all.★

He never failed to respond with enthusiasm to the evident expressions of love and faithfulness that came from every section of the Movement and he retained a deep affection for Chiara, whom he received twice in private audience and to whom he sent numerous messages of appreciation.

★ 'Città Nuova', no.6, 1975, p.42.

Pope Paul VI was much concerned with unity and Igino Giordani was often with him. Nearly all the Movements for unity today which have involved direct contact with the Roman Pontiff were initiated during his time. It was in his pontificate that the dialogue between Protestant and Catholic was taken up publicly for the first time since the Reformation. The occasion was a much heralded one in Geneva, when Cardinal Bea and Marc Boegner, head of the French Reformed Church, both spoke. Subsequent to that meeting, Marc Boegner had had many private conversations with Pope Paul VI. Between the two men there grew a deep affection and in more recent years a memorial has been placed on the Mount of Olives by Marc Boegner's son to mark those historic meetings. There were others with leaders of other parts of the Church. Throughout this period, Chiara and all the Focolare Movement, together with Centro Uno, directed by Igino Giordani, carried out an ecumenism that was encouraged by the Pope. The regard with which Paul VI was held by the other Churches is illustrated by the message sent to Cardinal Villot from the World Council of Churches, on 7th August 1978, the day after Pope Paul died. The message said that the fifteen years of Pope Paul's pontificate would 'be remembered as a decisive period in the life of the Roman Catholic Church and in that of all the other Churches. In these years the foundations of a new and lasting communion between all the Christian Churches has been laid'.

Pope Paul VI died in that year and Igino, although still eagerly involved, was advanced in years. He saw three Popes in that year, 1978: 'Peace, goodwill and a smile', he commented, 'was the hope generated by Pope John Paul I in his few days of office. His death was mourned by all the Churches and by the leaders of non-Christian religions'.*

* Serving Each Other, art. in 'New City', January 1979.

But Igino Giordani saw even in the sadness of that year a hopeful sign. 'The death of two pontiffs, Pope Paul VI and Pope John Paul I has saddened almost all mankind', he wrote in his article for the Week of Prayer for Christian Unity at the beginning of the following year. 'As a witness to their activity in the ecumenical field their death has shown the moral unity of mankind; a unity focused on these two men who were the spiritual and social leaders for the good of all men. Their funerals also had an ecumenical dimension and showed to the followers of different religions and ideologies and to non-believers, a centre of unity'.★

The other religions

In 1977, despite his age, Igino Giordani travelled to London to see Chiara Lubich receive the Templeton Award for progress in religion. He rejoiced at the enthusiasm with which she was received and saw something of her new vision. She declared openly that she saw a new step in the gathering into unity the people of other religions which she had seen in London. Once again, Chiara was marching in step with the Vatican whose eyes were also open to the non-Christian world. Before her biography was written and Igino had translated it into Italian, he had noticed and commented upon the newly formed Vatican Secretariat for Non-Christian religions. In that same article for the Week of Prayer for Christian Unity (1979), he broadens the range of prayer by reference to this Secretariat and its latest Bulletin:

> It contains studies of African religions and a report on discussions held in Kinshasa. These studies open up a

★ ibid..

new world and give a daring vision of how to approach different cultures while seeking the unity of an African Christianity. There is also an examination of the possibilities for collaborating with Muslims in the field of justice and peace, emphasizing what is held in common, and it shows how common values have been obscured in the past because of racial and political enmity.*

These are hardly the words of an old man, surveying and consolidating his life work. He is still excited by new ventures and ready to think afresh.

A few years before, Ignaz Maybaum, the distinguished Liberal Jewish teacher in London, had published his appeal for a 'Trialogue' between Jew, Christian and Muslim (published in the 'Littman Library of Jewish Civilization', 1973). Igino saw the importance of that appeal and inevitably linked it with the work of the Graymoor Franciscans in the USA and the *'Nostra Aetate'* (1974) of the Second Vatican Council which led to the setting up of two commissions, one for the religious relationship with Judaism, the other for Islam, both linked to the Vatican Secretariat for non-Christian religions. Igino also reviewed the special issue of 'The Journal for Ecumenical Studies' (Vol. XIV) which contained talks, articles and various texts documenting the discussions between the three religions. All this material was eagerly discussed at Centro Uno and with visitors who came to see Giordani at Rocca di Papa. Of course, as all three admitted, unity is a far off goal, but Igino saw 'an immense desire to love each other, to collaborate together, to search for a meeting together in the faith in the one God.'†

It was an ambitious vision with all the hatred and injustice of history against it, but Igino Giordani's

---

* ibid..

† *Tre religioni a confronto*, art. in 'Città Nuova', no.12, 1978, p.27

confidence in the power of love was unshakeable. He believed in miracles! After all, all three had Abraham for their father, all three venerated Jerusalem as the Holy City. And he went on to examine more deeply the possibilities for unity: 'The Koran teaches that faith does not express itself in turning to East or West in prayer, but in love for God by helping orphans and those in need, by exercising justice and freeing slaves, in fact by works of mercy as enunciated in "The Book". It teaches a conduct of human behaviour which according to Ansari could lead to mutual appreciation and to useful collaboration between the three religions'.* He points out that 'you must love your neighbour' is also a common duty in all three.

He does not deny the difficulties and he clearly recognizes how far these three religions are apart. But they have never been close and now there is a beginning. 'For the first time we are beginning to establish a relationship of friendship, which could lead to understanding and to collaboration between Mosques, Synagogues and Churches'.† He notes the representatives of other religions are also beginning to overcome their prejudices and difficulties, quoting with approval and urging upon his fellow Catholics the words of Hassan Saab, a Lebanese Muslim: 'The Catholic Church which has in the past concentrated on its own truths is turning for the first time to investigate the truths of other religions; it is presenting Islam as a sister religion, and exhorts Christians to eliminate every bit of discrimination, not only against Jews, but also against all non-Christians'.‡

And Centro Uno with Igino Giordani directing was at

* ibid..
† ibid..
‡ ibid..

the centre of this new educational process and he caught the vision. He was thus ready to hear the words of Chiara after she received the Templeton Award:

After my speech in the Guildhall, I had the impression that all of us present there were one, even though we belonged to different religions, almost as though Jesus' prayer, 'May they all be one', had been fulfilled. I asked myself afterwards what was the cause of this. My answer was, perhaps it happened because we all believed in God and in that moment perhaps God enveloped us all . . . the first to come and greet me were persons of other religions. A Lama came up to me, gave me his visiting card and told me he would write to the Dalai Lama of Tibet who is now in India, so that he could immediately contact me. Then four Jews came and said with joy that basically the Old Testament is the trunk upon which the New Testament is grafted, almost as if they wanted to tell me that therefore our Movement too has the same roots. Then three Indians came; they were Sikhs, as they explained to me, members of a religious movement that has spread all over Asia, born four centuries ago from the attempt to unite Hindus and Muslims in the faith in the one God. Their High Priest in England was there in the hall. They spoke to me describing their efforts to combine the two religions, convinced, I think, that this would please me because like us they are also working for a greater unity between people of different faiths.*

Igino Giordani did not live to see the development of relations with the Buddhists. This was left to Chiara and the Templeton Prize played its part. Nikkyo Niwano, President of the largest lay Buddhist Movement in the world, Risshō Kosei-kai, received the Templeton Award in 1979. He already knew Rome and on his way from London to Tokyo after receiving the Award, called on Chiara. Igino saw something of this development between

---

* *A Londra s'è aperta al Movimento dei Focolari una prospettiva nuova* [In London a New Perspective was Opened to the Focolare Movement], art. in 'Città Nuova', no. 8, 1977, p.30f..

the Risshō Kosei-kai and the Focolare Movement, but it was left to Chiara to visit Asia and in December 1981 take a new step forward in the dialogue with Buddhists. Chiara's Asia visit, which has been so well described in 'New City' by Enzo Fondi, consolidated relations with the Risshō Kosei-kai, whose leaders are very keen to open
up dialogue with other religions.

Igino and Chiara

We have been concerned in this chapter with Igino Giordani and the international dimension which he brought to the Movement and the Movement nurtured in him. It has been impossible to tell this story without constant reference to Chiara. The reason is that she is at the heart of the Movement. Where Igino has used his consecrated mind and learnt how to love; she has been the loving heart, going out to others. Her spontaneous approach to other religions is a good example of this. Igino carefully thought his way through to a desire for unity and often arrived at the same conclusion as Chiara by different routes. She recognized this when she referred to him as a 'co-founder' of the Movement. They influenced each other: she opened her heart to the wider possibilities of the Movement; he applied his mind to the tasks of the Movement. Yet it did not continue to be a separation of heart and mind. He learnt to love in a new way. Chiara explains this learning in an article contributed to 'Città Nuova' after his death:

A Christian of the first order, a scholar, an apologist, an apostle. When it seemed to him that he came upon a spring of living water, gushing up from the Church, a new testimony that the Holy Spirit is always alive and active in her, he knew how to sell everything to follow

209

Jesus who called him to quench his thirst with that water.*

Chiara and others have frequently commented on how extremely sensitive he was to the signs of the times and he was able to relate the Movement to the new signs emerging from the Second Vatican Council. Undoubtedly, his immense love for God coupled with his great intelligence and the breadth of his culture, enabled him to be a flexible instrument of the Spirit, giving no small contribution to unity.

Before dealing with two other parts of the Movement to which Foco made major contributions – the New Families Movement and the New Humanity Movement – which must occupy the next two chapters, we must record a comment of Mario, his oldest son, who is a distinguished surgeon. Two weeks before Igino Giordani died, Mario was with him and heard him speak of 'mutual love' and 'the unity of all Christians'.

Mario commented to the young doctor nearby: 'This is the moment of truth. A man in his condition speaks of the things he lived for all his life. You can tell that he lived for the unity of Christians'.†

* *Igino Giordani, focolarino*, art. in 'Città Nuova', no.9, 1980, p.23.
† Art. in 'Living City', New York, July 1980, p.6.

4

The New Families Movement

Once Igino Giordani had shown that there could be a married focolarino, the influence of the Movement upon family life had new possibilities. In harmony with what the Second Vatican Council was to affirm a few years later, when it spoke about the call of every human person to sanctity, the married state no longer represented an obstacle to striving after Christian perfection – neither for Giordani nor for the many others who followed him immediately afterwards. Chiara Lubich's living rediscovery in 1943 of the supreme Christian value, which is love, and the true vocation of every Christian, that is God, who is to be loved, 'with all the heart, soul, mind, strength', harmonized quite naturally the various spiritual gifts understood to exist in the Church: priesthood, virginity, consecrated life etc.. And precisely within this relationship of mutual respect and appreciation, where each of the spiritual gifts was fully accepted, every person felt powerfully drawn to live out the Gospel ideal of love. Giordani, who often repeated John Chrysostom's words that the laity should be like monks in everything except for celibacy, grew in joy as day by day he saw that his yearning for holiness had opened the way to a multitude of married people who shared in the same life and experience of God as those who remained virgins.

It was a return, in a certain way, to the origins, to the simple practice of Christian life, without all the trappings and the complicated divisions of the spiritual life that in the past had hampered the impetus of the lay person's love for God. But this growing number of people, the married focolarini, could not remain 'solitary', as it were: in the wider ambit of the Movement they had 'to bear much fruit'. In 1967, their fruit ripened in the birth of the New Families Movement.

According to the intuition of Chiara Lubich, its founder, this new Movement had to answer the needs of the family today. Its task was to bring the family back to God's original plan for it, by helping to heal the wounds of families in difficulty and showing them the immense beauties of grace and holiness that God has placed in Christian marriage. Clearly this could be accomplished only by couples who thirsted for holiness and who were aware, because of a degree of spiritual maturity, of being God's instruments. It was the married focolarini who had this role. And this was the manner in which the New Families Movement began to work right from its beginning in 1967, with Igino Giordani, aided by the married focolarini, animating all that was done.

Of course the basis for all this activity was the effort to love God and a living witness to love for one another. Soon, however, this activity also took the form of training courses for marriage. These were followed by national and international meetings that demonstrated the kind of life people discovered within the Movement and, in particular, within the groups of the New Families.

The Day of the Family*

On 3rd May 1981, a vast gathering of 23,000 members from all continents and 36 countries met in the Palaeur, the Sports Palace erected in the E.U.R., Rome, for the 1960 Olympics. They were there for the *Giornata della Famiglia* (The Day of the Family). It was also a tribute to Foco, the first married focolarino, who had done so much to establish in the family, in a way similar to that of consecrated celibacy, the fullness of the Gospel ideal.

The name of Igino Giordani, who had been dead about a year, was often heard that day and half way through the programme Danilo Zanzucchi, one of the present leaders of the Movement, gave a brief presentation of the life of Foco with pictures of his varied career. That presentation simply underlined what we were all thinking. Foco was really present and speaker after speaker, from Chiara to the Pope, made mention of his rich influence.

Personal experience

In keeping with the tradition of this New Families Movement, it was not a celebration of the man, however great, but the recognition of the power of the Ideal in family life. And this was done by a series of personal experiences. Family after family, from Brazil, Cameroun, USA, Holland, Germany, Kenya, Korea, Japan, Philippines, England, France, Australia etc. etc., came to the platform and told their story, often with children present. They told of difficulties they had encountered and how their devotion to the Ideal had enabled them to come through. One consistent note was sounded

* cf. *'Effetti di un'incontro'*, Città Nuova, Rome, 1982.

213

throughout: marriage is not based upon the couple, but upon two responsible and conscious individuals. To have a true family you need, first of all, to base your personal life upon God, upon love, love authenticated by the cross. God is love and loves each one in a personal and exclusive way. It is necessary to believe in this love and reply to it by opening oneself up to others: 'It is this discovery which leads many to the understanding that God must be given the first place in their lives, that the relationship with him is the most important one and that all others must be engrafted into this one, from which they acquire their true meaning'.*

19th July 1967

Looking back, we can see the actual birth of the New Families Movement, which Chiara Lubich founded on 19th July 1967. The example and the energy of Foco had contributed much to its birth. He soon gave to it a powerful lead. At the opening of its first conference, Chiara had said: 'To stress the value of the great sacrament of marriage and to make it bear the greatest possible fruits' was the aim of the Movement. Ever practical she asked the married focolarini, who were the Movement's driving force, how they would be able to make it be born, and she herself replied quite simply and profoundly: 'You need to live well in your own families and to have in your own family life the experience you take to others'.

Chiara recognized the power of love in the relationship between husband and wife and related this to God in a way that did not diminish it, but give it its true identity

* Art. in 'New City Supplement', June 1981, p.3.

214

and guarantee its fulfilment. When her friend was about to get married, she wrote:

> Listen to me: Do not divide your heart on earth, do not divide your love! There is only one love, only one: *Love for God*. . .
>
> He lives in the hearts of all creatures. But you, because it is His will, you must see Him above all in one heart: in that of M.! . . .
>
> Understand me: For you, love for God is to be shown thus: loving M. *as much as you can:* for Him deny your selfishness, your wish to stay closed in on yourself, your comforts, all your shortcomings. For Him increase your patience, perfect yourself as a mother, know how to keep silence when someone slips up! . . .
>
> Joys will come to you, sufferings and anguish will come. But if you force yourself to see Jesus in him . . . then your love for him will have no end . . . Only thus will your love grow to be gigantic.

So far as Foco was concerned, the great thirst he had had for God since youth, refined by culture and by experience, brought about a balanced personality. His family life, too, was filled with the divine. He had already shown in his charming little book *'La repubblica dei marmocchi'* ('The Toddlers' Republic') that he understood the rights of each individual within the family. In a section added in 1944, when war was at the gates of Rome, something can be glimpsed of his character and the life of his family. In a brief sketch, describing a family party to celebrate his sister's birthday, he tells of the noise and disturbance caused by the sheer exuberance of the children and the peace at the end of the day, when it is all over. Then he meditates upon the family as similar to the structure of an atom. It is not the old view of a solid, indivisible atom, impregnable by outside forces, but of the modern discoveries about the structure of the atom with a nucleus, protons and electrons. He compares the electrons moving at great speed around the nucleus to the children running through the corridors of the house! Then his love for his children shines out, and he writes:

> It is life. And it reacts . . . with gurgles of laughter against the pressure of steel, of explosives, and of stupidity, which are used, on every side, by death. Not for nothing, in the eyes of children, laughs the light of God, who is the God of the living and not of the dead, as was said by Jesus, friend of infants.★

That may sound sentimental, but we must read it in the noise of battle and with Igino's memory of destructive war. He already knew how to learn from the freedom of his children and the love of his wife. Marriage barred him from celibacy, but not from love, love of Mya and love of God. Chiara helped him to see more deeply into family love as part of our love of God. She told him of her own experience in Loreto, where she had so deeply felt the presence of the Holy Family in that 'sacred house'.

There is an entry in Foco's 'Diary of Fire', for 10th January 1960, which illustrates both what he had learned from Chiara in this matter and the basic principles upon which the New Families Movement was founded some years later:

> If the family became aware of its sacrament and developed it . . . that is, if in addition to carrying out its functions in regard to birth, work, illness and care, entertainment and anxieties, it fulfilled also its sacramental role as the organ for transmitting divine life, in addition to physical life, and as copy of the household of Nazareth, so that the father was Christ and the Mother the Church and the child was Christ-Church; if it were in the world as a representative of the Eternal, as the Church giving Christ to men and making of its fellowship a participation in the Trinitarian fellowship of God in heaven, realizing unity in trinity (father, mother, child = a single heart and a single soul), then

★ *'La repubblica dei marmocchi'*, op. cit., p.302.

216

its course on earth would be a repetition of Calvary, that is, it would bring forth redemption and resurrection.[*]

Marital ethics

On 29th July 1968, about a year after the formation of the New Families Movement, Pope Paul VI published his Encyclical Letter, *'Humanae Vitae'*, which condemns all forms of artificial birth control. This publication caused a wide variety of reactions. Particularly during his visit to Latin America, there were those who hoped that the Pope would recognize the connection between poverty and population, and rethink his teaching. *'Humanae Vitae'* was, however, quite firm. The Focolare Movement, and the New Families Movement, following the teaching of the hierarchy, made it their own. It was not in the nature of the Movement to compromise, so it carefully supported the Papal Encyclical by a wise teaching on family life and the attitude to birth.

In the first 'New City Supplement', published in London in June 1981, the teaching on birth in the family is clearly set out:

When there is love the decision to space the birth of children or to avoid it, is made only if it is for the good of the entire family and its individual members. In an environment of true love based first of all on a spiritual communion, the true value of abstinence is discovered. If it is true that love is nourished by physical intimacy, it is also true that love grows where periodic continence is practised out of love. Couples have discovered here something more than a method, rather a Christian way of life, both human and humanizing. This has been the experience, thirteen years after the encyclical *'Humanae*

[*] *'Diary of Fire'*, op. cit., p.71.

Vitae', of couples from many countries all over the world with whom the New Families Movement is in contact and who have started to live in the way it proposes.*

It is no surprise to learn that Igino Giordani was opposed to all forms of liberalizing the abortion laws in Italy and that the 'Day of the Family' in Rome on 3rd May 1981 launched a message, as well as proposing models of life, opposed to all that had brought about the passing of laws in Italy that liberalized the laws on abortion. What the Focolare most particularly felt must be corrected is an attitude to life that made abortion more or less a form of birth control.

Mary and the family

Some of the most valued testimonies to Foco's contribution to the Focolare Movement come from families.

Much earlier, he had seen the role that Mary plays in this new attitude to the family upon which the New Families Movement is based. Like Chiara, he saw the value of the model of the home in Nazareth where Jesus had been brought up by Joseph and Mary. Foco wrote a great deal about the Virgin Birth, but still more about the motherhood of Mary and her family life. There is no sentimental piety in the Focolare Movement's relationship with Mary, but it is founded on the New Testament account of this remarkable servant of God. She is seen particularly, as Chiara puts it, as a model to imitate and to relive in one's own life.

The example of Mary is paramount in his understanding of the spirituality of the married state. In an article written for the American Focolare magazine in 1962, he

* Art. in 'New City Supplement', June 1981, p.6.

218

insists upon the virginity. She is 'a virgin who became a mother while remaining a virgin, who wishes today that mothers and fathers, while remaining as such in the midst of the world, should in turn attain to spiritual virginity'. He describes in N.T. terms how Mary, despite her natural tendency to a contemplative life, 'dedicated herself to ordinary practical activities'. She was for Foco the model of the person consecrated to God, belonging wholly to him, full of the Holy Spirit, yet immersed in everyday tasks. ' A woman like so many others'.

It was the same with Joseph. Like Chiara, he saw Joseph as devoting his whole life to Mary and Jesus. 'Mary and Joseph', he wrote in that 1962 article, 'are the two models for lay persons, consecrated to the Lord'.★

With this high view of family life, he could see that consecrated married people represented God's strategy for the overcoming of evil in the world. It was not difficult for Foco to find from his stock of reading many examples of saints and fathers of the Church who supported his thesis, but eventually he turned to one of the encyclicals of Pius XII.

Consecratio Mundi

In his biography of Pius XII, *'Un Grande Papa'*, published in 1961, Igino Giordani points out that in the Pope's battle against the forces of evil, he called for a reconsecration of the world to God. For this task, he mobilized the love of the laity for Christ 'in their conscience, in the families, in their morality, in civil order and in international co-operation'. Igino explains the main thrust of

★ Art. in 'Living City', New York, 1962.

this drive from the Pope in Focolare language! It is the offer of love, a 'wise love, which is considerate of the sinner, but not of the sin'. He calls this a love which is like the flame of truth. The chapter that follows on 'The Santification of the Laity' is a powerful exposition of the encyclical and bears many traces of the influence of the Focolare Movement. What is clear throughout is that Giordani, the 'Foco of the Focolare' has already proved the intellectual basis, grounded in the teaching of the Fathers and of Pius XII, for two Movements yet to be formed in the Focolare Movement – 'the New Families' and 'the New Humanity'.

He consistently based his arguments upon the example of Mary, the fathers and mothers of the Early Church (lay people who consecrated themselves to God and lived for him alone, who did not impoverish their lives by the pursuit of material goods), the sanctification of the religious orders, the saints, and of course St. Catherine of Siena among them. In that 1962 article he describes how the Popes in modern times tried to mobilize the laity through Catholic Action. Then turning to Pope Pius XII and commending the encyclical, *'Consecratio Mundi',* he describes it as meeting the need to re-consecrate the world that has been paganized. And this task of consecration he sees as entrusted by the Pope to the laity. 'It would seem', he concludes, 'that our Movement is one of the Movements destined to contribute to the *Consecratio Mundi'.*

Foco took the logical step of comparing families with the family at Nazareth. The key passage is:

We must organize human society in such a way that priests, virgins and married people, should manifest, together, the living Church, and should thus attract others to the truth. In Jerusalem there formed round our

220

Lady a community in which all were of one heart and mind. The obligation to do this is still valid today. To a great extent it is up to us married people to make the house of Nazareth, the house of Mary, exist once again on earth, with Jesus in the midst, and his mother close by.*

'Fui il primo papà di famiglia focolarino'

That was Foco's repeated boast, which he always said with a playful smile: 'I was the first focolarino who was the father of a family'. While admiring the virginity which was an essential part of the Focolare Movement, he tried to open the way for married people. He felt himself called to an original kind of vocation, just as Chiara had in her earliest days when no accepted form of religious order suited the call she had received from God. Hers was a way of perpetual virginity, but Foco discovered a vocation which might be called a 'spiritual virginity'. He saw the real value of the family in the spirituality of the Focolare Movement.

With Foco, then, in a Movement that stressed charity more than virginity, it was possible to 'expand the walls of the convents and monasteries', as he himself said. Working in unison with Chiara, he contributed greatly to this 'expansion', although he did not have a position or organizational leadership in the New Families Movement. He spoke of it in an editoral he wrote which shows his care for the preparation of young couples for marriage. It appeared in the issue of New City for May 1980, the month after he died:

The Christian woman in our times, even though vices

* *'Pius XII: Un Grande Papa'*, SEI, Turin, 1961, pp.667–670

and errors abound, presents herself as the image of Mary, which means purity, beauty and joy.

This is what a woman is created for, to give back fullness and dignity to human existence so as to create a shared life in which the will of God is lived in every form of activity, and this is a very important aspect of the universal priesthood to which all the baptized are called.

An 'angelic' formation in childhood opens out the souls of the adolescents, removing many earthly obstacles. Children, if they are formed with love, are aware of these essential values of life.

The result is wonderful when they understand that they represent Jesus, that they too are Jesus, for their brother, for their family for all of society.

Both inside and outside the home, the domestic church, when marriage is lived in this way, continues as the new commandment of love, achieved daily, a constant source of strength and unity in trials and in joys.

Through this kind of marriage, each family home becomes a fire which burns, even when the surroundings are icy.

Marriage is the structure for collaborating with God in order to create life; and God is life. This shows us how sacred is the value of created beings in the world who have totally given themselves in the world and act for the vitality of the world. We see how great the dignity of man becomes if he knows how to act according to the Creator's plan. . .

In the family, the husband and the wife and the children are united by the sacrament in the unity which Jesus lives with the Father, and with the Holy Spirit, because as the Father established: 'Therefore a man leaves his father and mother and cleaves to his wife and they become one flesh' (Genesis 2:24) and they are one soul, they are united permanently.

Therefore 'what . . . God has joined together let no man put asunder' (Matthew 19:6).

Testimonies

The New Families Movement proceeds by personal contact, as is common to all parts of the Focolare Movement. The families meet in groups to share with one another how they have lived the Gospel; they go to Mariapolises; and they organize courses. Married couples are encouraged to speak of their experiences, talking freely of the problems they have faced in their marriage and how they have overcome them. The stories are not of easy success. They are frank and often include divided families, where only one of the partners is trying to live the Ideal. They are very moving.

This chapter must conclude with a few detailed testimonies. They are taken from those heard in Rome at the 'Jubilee of the Family' in 1984.

Experience of Emile and Madeleine Gahie-Koissi (The Ivory Coast)

Emile:
Even though we were baptized, Madeleine and I did not go to Church. We already had children. There was no room in my daily life for forgiveness. For me, to forgive someone's mistake meant to consider that person inferior to myself. Therefore, I did not accept apologies from any one. Moreover, my pride did not allow me to ask forgiveness of others. This attitude of mine made the atmosphere of my young family unbearable, especially for my wife, but I wasn't able to do otherwise.

Madeleine:

My husband's way of acting hurt me in the innermost part of my being. He did everything his own way and if someone asked for an explanation, he answered harshly.

My sadness increased day after day. I wanted to leave forever. I was actually packing my bags when my husband walked in and in his usual arrogant way, he said to me: 'Where are you going woman? Why wait until tonight to leave? Go at once!'

I became even more irritated. I sent half of my luggage to my parents. While I was putting some papers on my desk in order, I came across a sheet of paper with this verse from the Gospel: 'Love your enemies, bless those who hate you'. I sat on the bed. I took two deep breaths. The sheet of paper also had a comment on that sentence from the Gospel. I read it attentively. Then I went to the refrigerator and drank a large glass of water.

I reflected for a moment: *In my case, who is the enemy whom I must love? Who is it that hates me, that I must bless? The answer flashed to my mind at once: 'The one who makes you suffer.' My husband, then.*

I thought: *If I must be ready to love my enemy, even more so must I love the father of my children.* I decided to stay. I brought my things back to the house, but above all I decided to change my attitude, my way of behaving. It was difficult, but I wanted to try.

When my husband returned home, I greeted him. I offered him something to drink and asked him if he wanted to eat. I did the same in the following days. In other words, I learned to be attentive to him.

Emile:

Madeleine and I have come back to the Church. We got married in Church and I returned to the sacraments: Penance and the Eucharist. Little by little, I began to understand the meaning of forgiveness. I found the courage to forgive wrongs and also to ask for forgiveness.

Now there is trust between my wife and me and with our children. I believe that this reconciliation has taken place only through the grace of God and every day we make the effort to jealously hold on to the harmony which now reigns in our family.

Experience of Ivet Inocento (Philippines)

I am the fifth child in a deeply Christian family of eight children. Our parents had already educated us according to their principles, and had begun to encourage us to attend meetings in Christian environments, in their desire to give us the best.

As the years passed, many questions arose within me. I asked myself what the real sense of life was; I knew only one aspect of it, that which my parents had shown me. I felt very limited. I wanted to know many things, to experience them; to be free, to personally discover my way.

I left the usually 'good' company that I had, and made friends with other young people.

I always came home late. My mother waited for me in the evenings, but she never scolded me. My father offered me advice, but he did not weigh me down.

Being able to rely on their love gave me security. For me they were a constant source of help.

I studied a lot during the examination period; but as soon as I could, I would go around with my friends, ready to meet all kinds of experiences: alcohol, smoking, drugs.

Months passed. At first I was happy. But soon, I

started to feel insecure and, seeing my parents, I began to ask myself if I was really doing the right thing.

Their example and constantness, their disinterested love finally touched me. I took the opportunity to play the drums in a meeting of young Christians, determined to start a new life.

A relationship of profound communion was born between my parents and me, leading me to the total choice of God. But I was not the only one in my family: my other four brothers and sisters have also given their lives to God.

The true freedom

The New Families Movement has been deeply concerned with the problems of broken families, not only for the effect upon husband and wife, but increasingly because of what it is doing to society.

Pope John Paul II said that the crisis in marriage (by the end of the decade, one in five of the couples married in 1983 will be divorced) is rooted in a wrong conception of freedom, in which one partner seeks, not the good of the other, but selfishly his or her own well-being.

Frequently, Igino Giordani insisted that marriage is of two individuals, who do not possess each other, but learn the true freedom by loving each other. It was the heart of his teaching and there are many places in his 'Diary of Fire' where he expounds his views on 'freedom':

> If a person does not wish to believe, he is free not to believe. God has impressed the seal of his greatness upon man by making him free. Only he teaches man to use freedom as freedom from evil and not freedom from good.*

---

* 'Diary of Fire', op. cit., p.116.

He maintains that the Lord shows us the other face of things, even turning what looks loathesome and evil into a help in our growth towards holiness. Applied to marriage this deals with the worst form of division, when husband and wife can become utterly hostile to one another. It is at this point that the Gospel injunction to love our enemies indicates a solution. In an apparently paradoxical flourish, Foco declares that when we look at Christ and see things in the light of Christ crucified, 'poverty becomes wealth, disgrace becomes glory, darkness is full of light'.

'We notice the evil men who seem to oppress us', he continues, 'become our collaborators; involuntary agents of our holiness. Ugliness thus becomes beauty, misfortune an opening to grace. History grinds like a noisy and dusty mill, from which flour issues; and from it bread is made'.*

There are no illusions in the vision that the New Families have of marriage, no romantic views of 'living happy every after'. Marriage has to be worked at in the light of Christ.

All this has to be taught before marriage or it will only be learnt in sorrow and often failure afterwards. Which is why Foco spent so much time writing and speaking to young people so that they would be well prepared for their future family life.

In the New Families Movement preparation is done through the telling of experiences. Principles are taught, as Jesus taught, through parables, parables from life.

A young girl describes how her engagement broke down and then was restored only after they had decided not to have sexual relations any more. They learnt not to possess each other, but to help each other to grow as people.

* ibid. p.117.

Another illustrated how difficulties rather than forcing the two apart created a stronger bond between them. 'This saved us from having too many illusions afterwards about our life as a couple or as a family'.

An editorial Comment in the Focolare magazine 'New City', for January 1984, speaks about the family in a way that is reminiscent of Foco's style and shows his continuing influence after his death:

It is generally agreed that the problems of society would diminish if children grew up in a 'healthy' family, in an atmosphere of love and security, and yet we continue to create conditions which tend to destroy what we should be upholding. The situation can be compared to a dentist who tells us how important it is to care for our teeth and who then proceeds to give us a prescription for toffee apples. Of course such a man would be considered to be mad and no one would give him credibility. Why then do we continue to give credibility to those who advocate an equally contradictory system in society? We could start to change this absurd contradiction, opposing any measures that further reduced the 'commitment' in marriage. Healthy families could give practical support and advice based on their own experience, without deluding anyone as to the difficulty of building relationships within marriage and within the family. Let us not delude anyone either about the beauty, the peace and joy, and the fulfilment which are to be found in marriage.

This chapter has spoken of Foco's unique role, in association with Chiara, as the first married focolarino and in relation to the New Families Movement. The next chapter will concern something else in which he had an important part to play: the New Humanity Movement.

5

The New Humanity Movement

The life of Igino Giordani does not proceed steadily forward like a fast flowing river, but if we are to keep that image, it fans out like a delta. We have recognized the development of a new spirituality, which was given new richness by the spirituality of Chiara; we have watched the international dimension enlarge in the Focolare Movement under the influence of his own international contacts; we have encountered a new sense of family life, which grew out of his own experience of marriage and the *tour de force* of joining the Focolare Movement as a married man. Each time we have had to go back to 1948, when he recognized the transforming power of the charism of unity which Chiara Lubich brought to her Movement and to the Church, and his own growing experience.

The spirituality developed when he was growing tired of the compromises of political life; the international dimension which he fostered in the Focolare Movement came at a time when he was opening up to the world after the isolation of war and Chiara was becoming aware of the wider implications of the gift that God had entrusted to her; the spirituality of the family was forced upon him as he was accepted into a community which prized virginity. He did not come empty handed to the

Movement, although at times Chiara had to call upon him to empty his hands. 'Throw away your books and live the Ideal', she would say to him. But he had a unique contribution to make in all three fields – spirituality, ecumenicity and family life.

There is one other field: his long involvement in politics. His diary makes clear that he was disgusted with the whole sorry state of affairs; but he had thought through the role of a lay Christian in the twilight world of political affairs. In this he was both a theoretician and a practical politician. His first original writing was about the social teaching of the Church and his basic concern was with that link between the human and the divine which was necessarily in the interest of mankind. He believed that the freedom and dignity of human beings had their origin in the acceptance of Christ in the general life of the public. His spirituality was not merely personal.

In one of his books called 'The Two Cities', which he translated himself into English in 1961, he attacked the pietism of leaving the acceptance of Christ 'in the most remote recesses of one's conscience' (p.332). He would not have this public acceptance of Christ considered to be intellectually invalid. Without this acceptance in public life, the freedom and dignity of mankind would 'drown in front of political absolutism and economic subjugation', he wrote. All his life – before and after 1948 – his main concerns were with freedom, legally guaranteed for all peoples and associations, equality, solidarity, the just use of material wealth, the dignity of work, harmony between Church and State, the morality of public and business life, anti-militarism and an advocacy of peace on the international scene.

Early development of Giordani's political thought

His earliest writings were sympathetic to the discussions of those Catholic Democrats who were the precursors of the Encyclical, *'Rerum Novarum'*, 1891, by Leo XIII, which dealt with Catholic social doctrine. He tended to favour the French Catholic thinkers, especially Lacordaire and Montalembert. His diaries reveal something of the anguish of the man trying to live up to these high ideals in the knockabout world of Italian politics after the war. He examines himself critically, admitting the inconsistencies between his own personal faith and his public life. He writes of how frail a personal Christian practice ('ascesis') can be, made futile by 'failures in politics, literature or social life'.[*] He writes of his distress at feeling powerless in fulfilling his own desires of 'Spreading sanctity by a poor sheet of newspaper [the reference is to 'Il Popolo', which he was then editing], spreading sanctity from a lobby of forlorn hopes [the halls of Montecitorio] . . . who will perform this miracle?' he asks in 1946.[†]

The meeting with Chiara in 1948 and the continuous contact with the emerging Focolare Movement began to give him hopes of an answer. It gave him a way to relaunch more powerfully his already ardent Christianity.

Christianizing politics

As Igino Giordani immersed himself in the new Movement and became an essential part of it, there was no diversion from his earlier political thought. Earlier he had lacked the energy necessary to carry forward what he

[*] 'Diary of Fire', op. cit., p.27
[†] ibid. p.24.

saw to be his mission – that of 'Christianizing politics'. A saint had done this in an earlier century, the fourteenth. Catherine of Siena, a virgin consecrated to God, had had the strength to influence politicians in order to 'heal and redeem an area of activity which, more than any others, is exposed to corruption, falsehood and ambition', as he said in his own book called, indeed, 'Christianizing Politics'.* In that book, he expressed his growing need for a revival in himself and in others of the spirit of the followers of St. Catherine. The spirituality of unity which he at once discerned in Chiara appeared to him like an enormous source of energy, useful in society as well as in the Church, in order to 'transform human society into a co-citizenship with the saints, so that grace may be introduced into politics, making it a tool of sanctity'.†

It was on this basis that Igino Giordani made one of his major contributions to the development of the Focolare Movement. He enabled the initially small group of consecrated people to become aware of the human efficacy of the charism of unity which could manifest itself in this way.

The volunteers

By joining the Movement, as its first married man, with all his range of experience and knowledge in so many fields, Igino soon became a symbolic reference point, as Chiara Lubich's spirituality expressed its great potential in ever more concrete ways.

This was how the branch of the volunteers emerged.

* *'Cristianizzare la politica'*, Rome, 1960; quotation from Giordani's own translation, 'Christianizing Politics', 1962, p.19f..
† ibid. p. 19f..

They were persons called to live and to spread the spirit of unity in the most disparate sectors and structures of society, contributing to the fulfilment of Jesus' prayer that 'all may be one' (Jn 17:21). And because of his deep spiritual life and his profound unity with Chiara, Foco in a sense represented the actualization of this development in the Movement.

Of course, there had always been a presence in society of members of the Movement, initially all consecrated people – focolarine and focolarini – because they were living in the world and doing many quite ordinary jobs. But their consecration as virgins in communities kept them apart from the structures of society in an organized way. With Foco not only did there come to exist an original form of consecration for married people, that later widened its horizon to the whole field of family life and its present-day traumas, but also the volunteers had an example in him as a politician, writer, journalist, who was deeply in love with God and open to every human interest, and had a great sense of unity.

This large group of people were certainly not second class citizens in the Movement, although they were not called to a consecrated life. They began to work side by side with the communities of those who were consecrated. They too had a vocation, differently defined. The volunteers were called to immerse themselves fully in the various activities of society – Giordani had shown that despite difficulties even a politician could do this – but be linked by the same Ideal, by that mystical reality which holds all of the members of the Focolare Movement together.

The volunteers could bear witness to the love of God and neighbour within the structures of society and thus renew interpersonal relationships in every sphere of practical life. In this vocation, they lived within the existing structures without ignoring the harshness and disharmony around them, which they did not accept passively.

Seeing the difficulties more clearly because they lived the spirituality of the Movement in all its Gospel richness, instead of passively accepting the pain of those harshnesses and disharmonies, they recognized in them an aspect of the mystery of the cross. And going out to Christ crucified, they found the strength to carry on loving and the light for a renewing urge. The goal of the volunteers indeed is to contribute to redeeming the structures of society as they now are and, as far as possible, to humanize them for the service of others. In playing their part in an attempt to transform society radically, they feel themselves to be in solidarity with all those forces committed to work in every field, from the cultural to the political, from the moral to the economic.

St Catherine's Centre

Such a task required co-ordination and nourishing. A centre was needed to provide ample opportunity for discussion and spiritual development. A centre, defined as both practical and theoretical, came into being in 1959. The plans were made, as so many plans are in the Focolare Movement, at a Mariapolis, held in 1959 at Fiera di Primiero on 22nd August. Igino Giordani and a few others concerned with the sanctifying of political life felt that this commitment should be consecrated to Mary. Chiara found the words to express it. As quoted by Giordani in 'Christianizing Politics', she had seen their need to 'entrust to Mary, Queen of all peoples, their political commitment.'*

* op. cit., p.40.

This gesture of consecrating all to Mary was immediately seen in practical terms, as is typical of the Focolare Movement. Thus the Saint Catherine Centre was born. It took its inspiration from the Magnificat. Again it is Chiara who finds the words: 'The *Magna Charta* of Christian social doctrine begins with the words of Mary: *"He has put down the mighty from their seat, and exalted the lowly; he has filled the hungry with good things, and sent the rich away empty handed"* (Luke 1. 52-53)'.★

There were other Members of Parliament at that Mariapolis in 1959 and they quickly saw what Igino Giordani had in mind. Their names were Tommaso Sorgi, Enrico Roselli and Palmiro Foresi.

Tommaso Sorgi, writing of that occasion gives an illuminating description of Giordani and his deep concerns at that time:

> It was in God's merciful plan that I also be present with Giordani and the other Members of Parliament. The project for this centre was formed in the hands (and the heart) of Igino Giordani, to whom I had been introduced a few years earlier by some people in the Movement. I had met him in 1956 at Montecitorio where he, no longer a Member of Parliament, had remained as librarian. I discovered him precisely along a 'corridor of useless footsteps', not in all his brilliancy as apologist and polemicist – as I had known him through his writings – but in the renewed gentleness and meekness of a prophet of love. This was an unusual reality to attempt to introduce into that area which was characterized by antagonism and indifference.†

The Saint Catherine Centre was the first centre of the Movement devoted to a Christian presence in social life. Its special emphasis was on politics. Later others were

★ 'Stirrings of Unity', New City Press, New York, 1964, p.31.
† Art. in 'Living City', New York, August/September 1980, p.4.

formed, concentrating on business and industry, social services and art.

A few years later they were co-ordinated into a single Movement called at first the Movement for a New Society. Today it is called the New Humanity Movement. This Movement has grown within the Focolare Movement and is rooted today in every continent.

Its principles are the same as those that presented themselves to Giordani when he saw opening before him a way for the realization of what he had always sought: the Christianizing of politics. He contributed much to it, he lived for it, his work and energy and vision provided its vital force. During his whole lifetime he had worked and fought for a social Christianity. He stood erect in the morass of politics with the stature of a biblical prophet, contesting every attempt to separate faith from works and against every 'murder of freedom'.* Giordani's vision was born of penetrating insights into the historical experiences of Christianity and his well-balanced reading of the Gospels. It is a view far removed from both an overly simplistic faith and a strategy which swallows up faith: it is open to a 'rational collaboration'.†

Such was the basis of the Saint Catherine Centre and in all essential ideas it remains the basis of New Humanity.

The Inner Conflict

Foco's private diary came out shortly after his death.‡

The published passages dealt mainly with his spiritual

---

* 'Le due città', Città Nuova, Rome, 1961, pp. 338–340
† 'La rivoluzione cristiana', Città Nuova, Rome 1969, p.70
‡ 'Diario di fuoco', op. cit., translated into English in the following year as 'Diary of Fire', op. cit..

development and the influence of the Focolare Movement upon his innermost feelings.

But there are some entries that bear upon the development of the New Humanity Movement even when he does not directly refer to it.

Shortly after the opening of Saint Catherine's Centre in 1959, he confided his growing thoughts about the 'new man' to his diary:

[1960:] *24th January* – Every time one opens a newspaper one reads reports and reflections on political disagreements, which are brought about by conflicts in economics and by various ambitions . . . And one learns of speeches and undertakings to restore order and re-establish unity, but with scant success. I am inclined to think that what is wanted is a charge of love, in a world in which selfishness carries all before it. Love would create the 'new man' afresh in all, would put Christ in all; and Christ is one; and politics would become the construction of the City of God.★

17th February – In the lobbies of the Chamber each deputy I meet relates misfortunes, and brings to light degrading facts. The press denounces corruption, lays bare scandals.

The result of speeches and reading is the realization that the dialectic of good and evil, even in the political sphere, or rather in it especially, confronts one with the dilemma; either to become a saint or shoot oneself. Two ways of liberation from evil, the outcome of social and spiritual disintegration. The choice is extremely obvious. One is Life – true liberation; the other is Death – final slavery.

But, although convinced of these truths, men as they grow older; they find toil increasing, irritations multiplying, solitude spreading like a desert, which as night falls, sees the last rare human shadows disappear. Love also sets, like a sun amidst clouds and the twigs of bare branches.

What does this mean? It means that the Lord creates silence around man, so that he can converse with him in peace and in depth . . .

★ 'Diary of Fire', op. cit., p.74.

Solitude therefore is to be seen as an invitation to recollect oneself more seriously and continually in the presence of the Eternal and to give value to the remnant of one's days by occupying one's mind in a higher contemplation with something better than electric domestic appliances, the day's news and noise.*

This entry must not be seen as an escape from the world of politics, however much he may have desired that at times. But, taken in conjunction with his activities in the Focolare Movement and the beginnings of The Saint Catherine Centre, rather as the seeking for the resources by which the Christianizing of politics may be accomplished.

The dedication to Mary was very important for Igino. In one moving entry he tells how he lost his way for a while:

17th March – I have been far from home and, drawn into the vortex of public engagements, I relegated the love of God and of the Mother of God to the fringe: and it was as if I had put out the light. Darkness came down on the road and rain fell: and anger and wrath sprang up like tangled brambles. The Mother was not there, and she did not switch on the light, she did not open the way to the Blessed Trinity, she did not escort the procession of the Saints . . . All at once I noticed my blindness and called out: Mary! And lo and behold a smile came back to my entangled and dripping soul, a patch of blue sky appeared, light returned.†

Describing this sense of loss which had come from trying to deal with political matters without the help of Mary, to whom he was dedicated , he writes on the same day:

I could not see Mary, I could not see even Jesus, in heaven, in my heart and in me, in my brothers: and therefore I could no longer see any brothers: I had entered the net of death.‡

---

* ibid. p.77f..
† ibid. p.80.
‡ ibid..

Igino could see that not all the problems were with the politicians. He was deeply distressed at what he found in the Church also. There would be need for change there too if the City of God was to be constructed:

21st March – The difficulties of life in the Church, the conflicts and at times the delays in the expansion of Christianity do not come so much from non-Christians as from Christians who are engrossed in the worship of money . . . Sanctity is in the end, and in the beginning, liberation from the shackles of money . . . The exploitation which paralyses religion is carried on beneath the sacred banners, by false Christians who want to defend privileges and accumulate capital. And the poor often mistake this semblance of sacred things . . . for true religion. If the spirit of Mammon takes possesion of the spirit of Christian individuals and groups, it immobilizes their feelings and turns their faith to stone. Instead of a living church, one has a sarcophagus.

Truly the most arduous part of the effort to attain sanctity consists in freeing oneself from this servitude.*

As the diary proceeds through the sixties, Igino records his reactions to the political turmoil of his country. He frees himself from ambition. He accepts the solitude and neglect. He is satisfied as he turns his whole attention away from man to God. But his concern for the renewal of his country remains and gradually he integrates his intense desire for inner sanctity with his longing for liberty and social progress.

[1963:] 12th July – Social progress is the fruit of religious awareness, which makes us see in man, our brother: indeed Christ himself. But religious awareness is favoured in its turn by social, cultural and political progress.†

The last entry in the published diary is for *1st December 1968*, when preparing for Christmas Foco meditates

---

* ibid. p.80f..
† ibid. p.96.

upon the nature of freedom. In that entry, we can detect his thoughts about that momentous year of student revolutions and the Russian tanks in Prague. The efforts by Dubcek to create a 'Communism with a human face' and the discussions between Christians and Marxists in the previous year awakened hope in his mind. The conference at Marienbad in 1967 showed what a believer could see in reading the signs of the times; the tanks in Prague is what the one-eyed man could see without faith. In this entry he sums up the philosophy of the New Humanity Movement.

In God man is free to love: that is to live; against God, he is free to do evil, that is to die.

He who seeks finds. He who seeks God, finds him. He who listens for him, hears him. His voice teaches us continually to reverse the current opinions in order to bring men and things firmly into the divine plan, which is immortality in beauty.

Illness torments: the man who accepts it in the spirit of Christ Crucified makes of it a chemical process of self-purification and a contribution to the Passion of Christ. A certain man is ungrateful odious: looking at him again with the eyes of our common Father, he becomes my brother, who needs my help. Certain words offend us: if we examine them in the light of God the Father, they afford us an opportunity for suffering and forgiveness, that is, for making a leap forward in the ascent which ordinarly perhaps would take years of reflection . . .

History . . . is an engine which, with earthly materials, war struggles, epidemics, hatreds and also with grain, water, metals and terrestrial energies, prepares for an approach to the spirit. And the whole of creation is seen, as it appeared to St. Paul, to yearn to converge on Christ, where the definitive grafting of human and divine, of earth and heaven, of matter and spirit, takes place.

The man who looks only at the earthly, fleeting, negative aspect, seen from this world, looking towards the human sphere, renounces the more extensive region of life: he becomes only an object of death, of which men and events make themselves the authors.

Christmas is drawing near. For a man who sees with only one eye what is approaching is cold, darkness and hunger. For the man who sees things in God, with both the human and the divine eye, the Redemption is approaching, which is joy, life and deification.

For him Christmas is an image of the paradox that the Redemption constitutes for men. It reveals the ways in which the heavenly Father acts, who makes of a stable the abode of the Eternal, the meeting-place of purity and beauty. He can make the God-Man come to birth in the bare and tattered dwelling of an old man, a person who is the temple of the Holy Spirit, if he wishes, and so a meeting-place for angels singing to the universe.*

Ten years on

The emergence of the New Humanity Movement after that first effort in 1959 with the formation of the Saint Catherine Centre was mainly in the sixties. It acquired new forms and in different centres different aspects of life were discussed and related to the spirituality of the whole Focolare Movement. During these formative years Igino Giordani was an invaluable guide. His knowledge of the world – politics, literature, social life – enabled him to advise from first-hand experience. He greatly enlarged the experience of life in the Movement, and his example encouraged others to follow.

Naturally he was most influential in the political and literary spheres. But as the volunteers and others of the Movement were drawn from engineering, education, art, medicine etc., other centres were formed – St. Giovanni Bosco for Education, Saint Luke for Medicine etc.

*ibid. pp. 116–118

In 1968, all these centres were united under one structure, called the New Society Movement and, later, the New Humanity Movement. It had a Central Secretariat, of which Giordani was not formally a member; but he was more than present in spirit, and the lines of thought were his. In fact, the Focolare Movement does so much in communion that it is difficult to find a difference of view! In a series of interviews several years after the formation of the New Humanity Movement, Giulio Marchesi and Claretta Dal Ri, who at that time had leading roles in New Humanity, answered some questions about the volunteers and their commitment in the social field. Giulio Marchesi clarified the nature of the New Humanity Movement, beginning by distinguishing it from the political parties and ideologically orientated social organizations that swarmed in Italy at that time. He said of these other movements:

> It seems to me that the 'political and social dynamics' or activities, nurtured by the associations that you mentioned, are a way of 'being society' and of regulating human society. They are not, however, the only way. Every now and then I notice in these activities signs of profound crisis, disillusionment and serious gaps that, as the situation stands, cannot be bridged. Humanity today is searching in other ways to be itself. Many attempts in all directions are being made . . .
>
> Ours is a Movement with a spirituality as its basis. It is not a political association, not even in the New Humanity Movement, which is one of its many expressions and the one that most deeply penetrates into worldly realities. Don't think, however, that the whole thing is up in the air, so indefinite that it is beyond reality, and quite out of touch with the concrete situations in which we live.
>
> On the contrary, the Focolare Movement did not come from a study of the Gospel, but rather from a daily discovery of what is contained there – a discovery which the first focolarine made by putting the Gospel into

242

practice . . . At the beginning, in its very seed, it [the Movement] constituted a new society. . .

The members who are now living everywhere throughout the world, and especially those directly involved in the life of our society, are people of our time. They have families, they work, they participate in recreational activities. They make all kinds of social, political, labour and welfare commitments. They experience as others do, the demands, difficulties, crises and hopes of today's society. They also feel strongly . . . that the lived message of the Gospel offers them a very different way of being men today, of living together among men, not only in Paradise, but even on earth, not just in Church, but even at the bank, in the factory, in the hospital and so on.

Hence, at a certain moment, came the awareness that all these people, since they are involved in the realities of this world, could exercise a transforming influence on civil society – not only an individual and sporadic influence, but the influence of a mass movement – if they were united among themselves with others in resolving their social problems in the evangelical spirit they had already experienced.*

That is how Igino saw it – as did all his brothers and sisters of the 'Ideal' – and that is how it has developed. No attempt is made to impose a political party or political solutions upon the members. The New Humanity Movement has long since recognized that a world Movement cannot have one political solution for all countries. This is a spiritual Movement and its members belong to all kinds of political associations. They have a political goal, but it is in the nature of principles and guidelines, worked out together in conference and sharing of experiences. Giulio Marchesi defined the political goal of the Movement in words that might have been taken from Igino's own writings:

* Lorit and Grimaldi, op. cit., pp. 65–67

243

It is the message of the Gospel, either forgotten or little known, and even less lived. Men, because they are the children of the same Father, who is Love, are brothers and must love each other. That is, they must find fulfilment of their individual personalities not by exalting themselves, but by losing themselves and giving themselves to others . . . We are all part of the same body, each in his own place, each with his own reason for existing at the service of others. Therefore the stronger members take care of the weaker ones; but all work with the strength and the charity that comes from God.*

Changing people and structures

The Gospel changes men and women and therefore the Focolare Movement has emphasized the changing of individuals and has accomplished much in this way. But neither Igino after his visit to Caux nor the New Humanity Movement which he inspired would accept the limitation of personal change only. It is not enough to say: 'Change the child and you change the world'.

When asked whether she believed that the New Humanity Movement should renew structures as well as men, Claretta dal Ri admitted that today's crisis was also one of structures and continued in words close to Igino's own views:

We hold that it is necessary to exert an influence in both directions by helping both men and structures to change . . .

The members of the New Humanity Movement . . . belong to organizations that work to give new structures to society. They make their active contribution in schools, in unions, in legislatures, in health care units, and so on.

* ibid. p.78.

244

We are aware, however, that there are cases where the structures themselves are not in need of change so much as the method of using them . . . It is important to regard structures not as rigid schemes possessing an absolute value, but rather as instruments continually being modified to meet the changing needs of man. *

The international character of the Movement gives it a broad and more complete outlook on the issues dealt with.

In the year that Igino died, Pope John Paul II addressed a mass gathering of the young people of the Focolare Movement (a *Genfest*) gathered in St. Peter's Square. He spoke to them about those who really make history and what he said would have rejoiced Igino's heart:

You must be the avant-guard of people on their way towards the 'new heaven' and that 'new earth in which righteousness dwells'. Those who know how to look at the future are those who make history. The others are dragged along and end up finding themselves at the margin of their existence, always bundled up in the network of their worries, projects and hopes which in the end reveal themselves to be deceiving and alienating. Only those who commit themselves in the present without letting it capture them, but remaining with the eyes of their hearts always aiming at seeking 'the things that are above, where Christ is seated at the right hand of God' can orient history towards its fulfilment. †

A winning formula

Wherever the Focolare Movement has gone, all over the world, the New Humanity Movement has gone too. With the revolution of the Gospel that this brings, there is, in bud, a social transformation.

* ibid. p.73.
† Art. in 'Living City', New York, August/September 1980, p.23.

It is only a beginning, but with solid foundations. A universal relationship that always brings fruit is initiated by going to the centre of the Gospel, loving everybody, always, as in a saying from the Early Church that Giordani often repeated: 'Seen your brother, seen the Lord'.

The members of New Humanity do not impose a religious view on those who have no faith, but together with others, in a social context, they rediscover the true nature and the profound need that is in every person. Its fundamental guidelines were laid bare by Chiara Lubich on 20th March 1983 at the Palaeur, Rome, when she opened New Humanity's first International Congress. There were about 18,000 people present from all over the world. At the end of the day, in a speech by Pope John Paul II, New Humanity's guidelines were given their final seal.

A history of the New Humanity Movement would take us well beyond the scope of this book. We may, however, take a recent example and hear again the voice of Chiara Lubich.

3rd June 1984

On that day, the New Humanity Movement held an International Congress in Rome on *Economy and Work*.

After recognizing that all Italy, many European countries and representatives from other continents were there, Chiara defined the purpose of the New Humanity Movement as 'to incarnate in all expressions of human life the Focolare Movement's evangelical ideal', she told of the origin of the Movement in war-shattered Trent and then proceeded to outline its principles. She ended that preamble with one of her popular texts: 'Seek first the kingdom of God and all these things will be added unto you'. Then she launched into the subject of the importance of the work:

However, if Jesus asks that we seek first of all the kingdom of God, this does not mean that he exempts us from work. On the contrary . . . we should have a very elevated concept of work simply because God himself considers it in this way.

While it is a fact that man, because made in the image of God, finds his fulfilment in communion with God, it is also true that this is not his only consitutive element. The Bible points out that it is also characteristic of man to provide for sustenance and to work.

Thus, man *must* work. This is so very obvious in the Ten Commandments, for example, where God wished to stress the fact that man should *not* work on the day of rest. Nor does he give a particular commandment in the Gospels. But to make us understand to what extent man is synonymous with work, the Word of God – become man – did not withdraw into solitude in order to meditate and pray in the thirty years of his private life . . . Rather he was a worker. It is clear then that for God, work is such an important aspect of man that if it were lacking he would have to consider man as being less man.

Also the members of the Focolare – like Jesus – earn their living by working. Indeed, since the Movement found its initial inspiration in the home of three workers – Jesus, Mary and Joseph (in the house of Nazareth transported to Loreto) – its members feel that in working . . . they fulfill the will of God.

Even the focolarini who are called to community life, must bring only one dowry with them on entering the focolare – that of being able to work and earn their living.

For them as for everyone, work will not be an additive or balancing factor in a life of prayer. But work will be their very life, in the sense that they do not have the vocation, for instance, to dedicate hours of adoration to God, but to offer him their work.

And although they are called in a rather special way to proclaim a great Ideal to the world, they must do so above all by 'doing', by working rather than by preaching and in this way they continue the private life of Jesus. They serve God as focolarini first and foremost by serving him as workers. If we should have to give a definition of them as focolarini, we would have to say: they are workers . . .

The communion of goods

These are two pillars upon which our Movement rests: to seek the kindgom of God and to work.

But we members of the Focolare Movement have our own particlar style in seeking the kingdom of God. We must seek it in accordance with the way God has pointed out to us. It is a way we travel along not each one by himself, but together. In fact, we feel that we are sons and daughters of an epoch in which the Holy Spirit is underlining the words which are a synthesis of the Gospel: 'This is my commandment: love one another, as I have loved you' (John 16:12), and is putting into evidence the unity which Jesus asked of the Father. In so doing, he is forcefully calling people to work side by side with others – indeed, to be with all those who so desire, one heart and one soul.

But this has important and noteworthy consequences. One example, typical of the members of our Movement from its very birth, is a practical expression which must be at the basis of every other activity and consideration concerning the use of goods and the solution to social problems. This practice is the communion of goods which is achieved by some members in a total way – they give all they have – and by other members through regular contributions of their surplus.

Because this practice touches each individual in a personal and very real way, it forms a more legitimate and fruitful basis for any other good and lawful method to guarantee an honest and dignified means of livelihood for all . . .

The primacy of man

The discourse, then, touches upon the primacy of man:

> And because we know how to walk through life united
> to one another, being one heart and one soul, we have the
> possibility of giving a hand to humanity today, so that it
> may reach very important goals.

The observation is made that man is subordinated to the
efficiency and production of the machine, and work takes
on an alienating character. This leads to the necessity of
transforming the structures of economic life according to
the directions of '*Laborem exercens*' (para. 9).

Chiara then goes on to say:

> But a second conversion must come into play here and
> must be made by all.

Man's social dimension

> In the name of God who created him, man must be aware
> of his sociality, of his social being, otherwise he would
> not yet be completely man. In fact, another of his
> constitutive elements, according to Genesis, besides
> communion with God, besides being called to provide
> for his sustenance and to dedicate himself to work, is
> sociality – his relationship with others – with the woman
> and with brothers.
>
> And we know what sociality means for God. It means
> to love others as ourselves. *As ourselves*, not less. Indeed,
> to love them with a love which, because coming from
> more than one person, becomes reciprocal and, because
> inspired by Christ, generates unity. Herein lies the
> meaning of what we stressed earlier, namely that we
> walk through life together being one heart and one soul.
>
> Our collective spirituality derived from the Gospel not
> only can contribute to, but can be of vital importance for
> finding solutions to the present problems of the working
> world.
>
> In this spirituality, man, and so every person in the

working world (from the owner to the administrator, from the director to technicians, from office workers to labourers), each person, in order to build solidarity with others, must love everyone in such a way that he or she becomes one with the others.

In this spirituality, mutual love leads to reciprocal understanding, to sharing the fatigue of others, to making our own the problems of others and to seeking solutions together. It leads to finding common agreements for new forms of organization in the working world. All come to share and participate together in the means of production and in the fruits and profits of labour.

With what consequences?

If previously, for example, for an individual labourer, industrialized work was synonymous with being crushed and deprived of his personality, with being unable to see in work the fruit of his intelligence and hands, now because he considers his own all that regards the others as well, work cannot help but take on meaning, indeed, a stimulating meaning . . .

Civilization of love

The working world itself is linked with all the other 'worlds' of human life – to the political world, to the legal structures, to health, education and so forth.

In order that work may regain full significance for the individual person, there must be a rediscovery of vast-scale social relationships. Indeed, since the economy of each country is linked to that of the other nations, a worldwide social awareness is necessary as the Pope also affirms.

But who is capable of helping man to fully achieve this and to regard himself as a member of this great human family . . . 'without denying his origins and his membership of his family, his people and his nation, or the obligations arising therefrom . . . '?*

* John Paul II, *Address to the International Labour Organization*, Geneva, 15 June 1985, para. 10

250

Who can accomplish this after man has shattered his union with God through sin, thus seriously compromising over and over again, communion with his brothers and sisters and therefore human solidarity?

Who is capable?

Only Christ, the Lord is capable; he who is so often relegated to private life – and only his supernatural and universal love – so often considered as something limited to prayer life – yet it is this which is really the indispensable leaven for the whole of human existence in its manifold expressions.

It is only with his love that we can build confidently a world of lasting justice and peace.

And as far as work is concerned, it is only with his love that egoism and hatred – often considered as an essential law of social life – can be eliminated.

It is with his love that working communities will witness how unity rather than conflict can truly improve work.

With his love the life of society itself will not be conceived as a struggle against someone, but as a commitment to grow together.

Hence only a new civilization based on love will be capable of offering a solution to the complex problems of the world of work.*

Chiara then developed the global awareness of the Movement and stressed that in working we are continuing God's work, ending with a more prophetic passage on a new heaven and a new earth which echoed the words of Foco describing the stable in Bethlehem as 'a meeting place for angels singing in the universe'.

* Economy and Work in the New Humanity Movement, art. in 'New City', August/September 1984, selected passages.

251

6

Giordani Among the Italian Writers

In 1984, some four years after his death, a street in Rome was named after him. It was a very appropriate street, not yet fully developed, but one where many families would live and the sound of children playing would be heard. As is the Italian custom with such streets, it was given the name, dates of birth and death, and profession: *Via Igino Giordani 1896–1980, Giornalista.*

I was offended at first, because I recalled the rows of his books – more than a hundred were written and nearly that number published. They included studies of the early Fathers of the Church, standard works on the Social Teaching of the Gospels, the Fathers and the Early Church, three substantial biographies, two of Popes, the other of a Prime Minister, novels, anthologies, studies of French Catholic writers and sociological studies of the Church and its pronouncements.

When I expressed my concern to the family, suggesting that *Scrittore* would have been better than *Giornalista*, his son said: 'No! He was a journalist'. Then I recalled the long row of bound copies of 'Fides', 'La Via', etc. His contributions to other journals and his editorship of several papers. The book that Gobetti had asked for in his early days, *'Rivolta Cattolica'* was, after all a collection of political articles, the work of a journalist. Writers and

253

journalists are both an essential part of the literary scene in Italy. There is no clear dividing line and one uses the name most characteristic of the 'writer'.

Giuliano Dego, writing of the Italian poet Salvatore Quasimodo when he was awarded the Nobel Prize for Literature, describes him in words that could be applied to a serious journalist and certainly apply to Giordani: 'To bear witness to man's history in all the urgency of a particular time and place, and to teach the lesson of courage', he wrote was the task of Quasimodo in his poetry. It was certainly Giordani's task in his articles and books, from the articles in *'Rivolta Cattolica'*, published in 1925 to *'Pensiero sociale della Chiesa oggi'* ('The Social Thinking of the Church Today'), published almost fifty years later.

It is either because of his treatment as a journalist and therefore topical rather than permanent, or because of his consistent Catholic emphasis, that he is omitted from most of the surveys of Italian literature. Those surveys, whether in Italian or in English (usually heavily derivative of Italian works) tend to concentrate upon experimental styles, especially under French influence, or upon social subject matter with left wing tendencies. Apart from Germany, it is true of most European countries that Church writers are usually ignored in general surveys of national literature and treated as special cases. They are put in a category which implies that they are determined by their preconceptions and therefore not free to enter the market place of literature. In the case of Giordani this was accentuated by his reputation for impregnable integrity. It was only after his death that writers and critics began to place this man in the context of Italian writing.

Carlo Bo

At the time of his death and at the several commemoration meetings and broadcast programmes, there were many who paid tribute to the various aspects of Giordani's life and work. Of special interest among the literary figures was Carlo Bo, the distinguished writer and critic. He spoke as a fellow writer and fellow Christian:

> I knew Giordani at the time of his writing for the 'Frontespizio'. And at once I admired the strength, the integrity and the intensity of his faith. I must say that in these fifty years he has remained faithful to the first principles of his faith, knowing how to interpret the times, assessing the changes with the help of his rigorous intellect and his passion . . . With the passing of the years, study and attention to the problems of the world inevitably led to the discovery of other principles and better choices, and finally we have seen him pass from the experience of life to the light of the Church, in the same faith, so that it is possible to say that he entered directly into the army of Christian love. Leaving his honours, his extraordinary power of spiritual inventiveness has issued in the welding together of thought and action to become one unique aspiration. There are not many examples of such consistency, proved day by day in the conquest interior peace.*

Giulio Andreotti

One of his colleagues in the Italian parliament, Giulio Andreotti, recalled his integrity in the Montecitorio:

> The wonderful facility of his writing; the extraordinary ability to pick out from the most disparate sources of Catholic writing the exact quotation; a sympathetic and spiritual participation in the analysis of Christian sociology;

---

* *Testimonianze*, art. in 'Città Nuova', no.9, 1980, p.17f..

by such qualities Igino Giordani was – by his many works – a master loved and admired in the days of our youth . . . Giordani at the Montecitorio was distinguished by his total lack of any kind of ambition, by fidelity to his commission, by the respect he showed even to his adversaries. He was – and everybody knew it – truly a man of faith . . . *

Guido Gonella

But one who had known him for fifty years, a senator of rare susceptibility, Guido Gonella, summed up his qualities as a writer and his wide interest most succinctly:

My memory of Giordani goes back to the years just after the first World War . . . We met for the first time in Rome, and spoke of Montalembert, an anthology of whose writings he had edited, with a valuable introduction, which even to this day is useful for all who wish to know about this apostle of Liberal Catholicism.

He was not only a desk man, but a man who loved his country, an Italian who served Italy sacrificially to the point of heroism. Those who value decorations must know that Igino Giordani was wounded in the war and wears the silver medal. And to those who cannot utter two words without mouthing the sacred name of 'liberty' and to those who drift along with the political trends of the day, note that the anti-fascist Giordani was dismissed and lost his job because of hostility to the regime . . . A person like Giordani could not remain indifferent to the political conflicts . . .

A superior spirit, he did not organize political currents, and this explains why in the last decades the memory of his work has been replaced by that of very modest personages.

He was a fluent writer, a dynamic one, with an unmistakable note of vivacity in his articles, many of

* ibid. p.18.

which would bear reprinting . . . Like many of those earlier champions he eventually retired from political life. In his personality there is represented a wonderful fusion of activism with something which can hardly be distinguished from the spirit of asceticism . . . His memory will only survive in our spirit as we take up the apostolic work of Igino Giordani.*

The judgement of his peers

These three quotations are from hundreds that appeared in the months after his death and at the various commemorations arranged by Italian Radio and TV, by the Focolare Movement and on occasions such as that when the street, *Via Igino Giordani* was named. One of the most impressive was that by Giovanni Lugaresi and that appeared while he was still alive, in the 'Osservatore Romano Della Domenica' on 31st March 1974. It is headed, *'Igino Giordani: un maestro'* and listed in the subtitles were the names of offices and accomplishments of this 'master':

Secretary of Sturzo
Collaborator in the 'Liberal Revolution' of Gobetti
Reformer of the Catalogue of the Vatican Library
Friend and Benefactor of De Gasperi
Scourge of Those who Distinguished between
    Private and Public Morality
Seeking Holiness while Involved in Politics
The *Focolarini* and the Young.

In his long article, Giovanni Lugaresi, shows how his writings have accompanied all the changes of his growth, from 'Secretary to Sturzo' to 'The Focolarini' and how in all the changes he retained the style of a 'master'. There is

* ibid. p.12f..

no doubt that Giordani was greatly honoured for his integrity. Many were grateful for his interventions in time of crisis and his courage as 'no respector of persons'. But what also emerges is the quality of his writing at all levels. He is a journalist, able to communicate and always ready to be topical. Even his writings about the Early Church are shot through with contemporary references. He makes the Fathers walk the streets and corridors of modern Italy. The Montecitorio hears the voice of Tertullian and the Church of the Second Vatican Council comes to grips with the apologetics of Justin Martyr because of his books.

What emerges from these judgements of his contemporaries is a man of complete integrity, whose writing was powerful in many different fields. The politically minded remember his anti-fascist writings and his articles at the time of the birth of Fascism and of the Popular Party. Those more concerned with the intellectual bases of political philosophy emphasize his work on Montelambert and his books on the Church-State issues. The more religious detect a new spirituality in his writings and even an early appeal for a reform of the Church, as for example in 'The Sign of Contradiction'. Most of all the theologically minded recall his standard works on 'The Social Teaching of the Church'. He is remembered as a librarian with considerable achievements, but as a scholar too, especially in the field of patristics. Those who watched him withdraw from politics have often written him off, but many others have seen a new life in his spiritual writings within the Focolare Movement. There are classics among these books. Since his death his Diary has been published and translated into English as 'Diary of Fire'. If this is read side by side with the many books that have issued from his pen since he became the first married focolarino in 1948, it is easy to detect a new spirituality and a strengthening of his hold upon his material. He becomes less polemic and more concerned to understand; he is less anxious to win an argument than to communicate the love of God to those who have not discerned it.

In earlier sections we have looked at some of his writings, but it might be as well at this stage to look at all his books in chronological order and assess the magnitude of his contribution to the literature of Italy.

The books

His first book was published in 1918. It was the product of his hospital studies, a description of two temples in Tivoli. A poem followed as the war came to an end, which meditated upon death.

These were student efforts, but soon, involved in politics he divided his writings between political and religious. And yet they were not divided. His treatment of Christian apologetics in 1923 linked very closely in his ideas with his book about the policy of the *Partito Popolare Italiano*, which appeared in the following year with a preface by Luigi Sturzo. The influence of the French liberal Catholics was shown in the books after the Second World War. But before that he had worked on Montalembert in the twenties and his first book on the French thinker appeared in 1925 with the title, 'God and Liberty'.

We have already devoted much space to the next book, *'La Rivolta Cattolica'* which showed the journalist in his early days. The importance of Gobetti's sponsorship as well as its danger has already been noted. This most important collection and incidentally the clearest evidence of his early anti-fascism, was republished in 1945

259

and 1962. In the same year, he also published the defence of Alcide De Gasperi against Fascist denigration. In the midst of this busy writing life he managed to work away at his studies of Early Church writers: *'San Clemente e la sua lettera ai Corinti'* ('St Clement and his letter to Corinth') came out in 1925, *'La prima polemica cristiana'*, ('The First Christian Polemic') in 1929, and *'San Giovanni Crisostomo'* ('St John Chrysostom') in 1929.

But by this time he had been to America and that stimulating visit produced a book about 'The sisters of St John the Baptist' *('Le Suore di San Giovanni Battista'*, 1929), the novel *'America Quaternaria'* ('Quaternary America', 1930), the anthology of American Writers *'Contemporanei nordamericani'* ('Contemporary North Americans', 1930), a study of the life and thought of 'Protestants in the Conquest of Italy', *('I Protestanti alla conquista dell'Italia'*, 1931).

His first important book is, as he himself recognized, *'Segno di contraddizione'* which we have already discussed. It was published in 1933, with subsequent editions in 1936, 1941, 1943, and 1964. It was translated into Spanish, French and Czech. Giordani was by now a name to be reckoned with, both in the political field and that of Church apologetics. The book was disturbing and led many to expect much from this young writer. His ability to think about old concepts in an original way awakened the interest of some of the best minds in the Church. His dependence in some way on Luigi Sturzo was obvious, but he brought a more detailed knowledge of the Early Church and documents than Sturzo did. He made good use of the finest library in the world to which he now had access.

His next important task was to write a formative book on the social teaching of the Church. He read extensively and brought his own political experience to bear upon the documents. Again, Sturzo's influence was considerable, but Giordani's detailed knowledge of the Early Church was evident. He documented many of the points that Sturzo had used rhetorically. The work came out in four volumes and in revised editions and translation remained a standard work all his lifetime. Priests had to read it in their studies, but it found a readership well outside the Church and soon made its persuasive arguments felt in the Italian Parliament. The general title was *'Il messaggio sociale di Gesù'* ('The Social Message of Jesus'), later altered to *'Il messaggio sociale del cristianesimo'* ('The Social Message of Christianity'). In turn it dealt with 'The Gospels', 'The Apostles', 'The First Fathers of the Church', 'The Great Fathers of the Church'. It was republished in many editions and translated into English, largely for an American readership. Later it was translated into Japanese and Spanish. The original publication date was 1935.

While he was in the Vatican Library not a year passed without one or more books being published. He ranged widely – a novel about Tivoli in the time of Hildebrandt, a meditation on the family, 'Catholicity', 'The Protestant Crises and the Unity of the Church', 'Paul, Apostle and Martyr' (a large edition of this in an English translation with many reproductions of famous paintings was published in New York for the *Daughters of St. Paul*, in 1946). An important work appeared in 1939, 'The Blood of Christ', which was much translated. Then in 1942, he returned to his work on the social teaching of the Church by editing the encyclicals dealing with this theme, *'Le encicliche sociali dei Papi da Pio IX a Pio XII (1864 – 1942)'* ('The Social Encyclicals of the Pope from Pius XI to Pius XII (1864–1942)'). Again this book ran into many editions. In 1956 it was already a reference book and needed to be corrected and brought up-to-date. As a supplement to this book he wrote, *'L'insegnamento sociale dei Papi dalle encicliche'* ('The Social Teaching of the Popes from the Encyclicals'). Until the end of the war, books continued to appear, many developing what he had written in articles in 'Fides'. They were mostly religious – some on the ecumenical movement, the laity, the relationship between priests and laymen, several short biographies. There was a political touch in *'Pionieri della Democrazia Cristiana'* ('Pioneers of Christian Democracy').

Giordani had always been a pacifist (right from 1915), not so much from deep religious feelings, but because he saw the uselessness of war. His speeches in Parliament show this as we have seen and he published in periodicals his conviction that war solves nothing. Then in 1946 came, *'L'inutilità della guerra'* ('The Uselessness of War') followed at once by a book on Social Preaching, called *'Padre Nostro'*. His *'Testi sociali della rivelazione'* ('Social Texts from Revelation') appeared the year before.

These small books were eagerly read and discussed. And in the midst of it all he wrote a novel: *'Proietti fa la rivoluzione'* ('Missiles make the Revolution'). His active mind would not let him rest as he struggled with the inevitable revolution which overtook Italy after the war. He had seen the chaos of 1919 from a hospital bed and could do nothing to prevent the disaster which befell his country. Fascism was now destroyed but he did not want to see a Communist and therefore atheist revolution. He wrote against this possibility in several small books and articles. He also did a brief survey of the history of Christian Democracy as the Christian Democrats took control.

He was already a skilled biographer when he tried his skills on Pius X, whom he called, 'A Country Priest', *('Un prete di campagna')*.

The Focolare Movement was already influencing his spiritual writings and among these the most important was a little book called, *'La divina avventura'* ('The Divine Adventure') which first appeared in 1952, published by Garzanti, Milan, but subsequent editions issued from the press of the Focolare Movement, Città Nuova. The sixth edition was issued in 1976, and there will certainly be others. For the Sisters of St. John the Baptist, he wrote a study of *Don Fusco*, their founder, who was almost contemporary with Giordani. This set the scene for his great literary biographies of contemporaries. The most famous of these were, Alcide De Gasperi (1955) and Pius XII (1961). He continued to write and as the influence of the Focolare Movement grew he blended with it. His later spiritual writings are totally at one with Chiara.

In the year of his death, *'Diario di Fuoco'* (translated in English as 'Diary of Fire') was published, followed in the next year by his sketch for an autobiography called *'Memorie di un cristiano ingenuo'* ('Memoirs of an Ingenuous Christian').

Of course, he translated and wrote innumerable introductions. His output was enormous and his literary reputation considerable. Political, historical, biographical, romantic – it was all there – but his greatest influence will lie with his spiritual writings. He wrestled with the problems of living a Christian life in Italy of the sixties and seventies. Some of his thoughts went into 'Difficulties of a Christian today' *('Difficoltà del cristiano oggi')*, but far more went into his conversations with members of the Movement and visitors who come to conferences.

Learning to live: the divine adventure

Giordani's addresses at meetings of the New Families Movement gave him opportunities of relating the spirituality he had received from Chiara Lubich to married life in a unique way. Many of these addresses appeared as articles in 'Città Nuova'. One such article was translated into English (many were) and published in 'New City' under the title 'Learning to Live'. It appeared in the issue for May 1983.*

The article opens with the strong statement that man's experience of life is a 'rich and beautiful adventure', because of the varied contacts with other people. Then he continues:

> The beauty of such an adventure is due to its link with supernatural life. In this link we find the strength to transfer our spiritual existence to heaven, or to cause heaven to come to earth: we find the strength in both cases to settle our spiritual existence on indestructible foundations.

This is supported by texts from the New Testament which show that the Christian through faith in Christ and the relationship of love with his brother, reaches the Father and with the Father's love unites himself to all mankind. This is the triangle which Foco finds in the New Testament and it is at the heart of Focolare spirituality: the two operations, reaching the Father and uniting with mankind, are compared to the two arms of Christ on the cross and they enable us to live a free life. We are no longer 'the servants of riches, consumerism, power, vice and hatred'. The two operations give light and strength to insert into human life the light of religion.

Foco shows the double effect of this opening of one's life to God and to our neighbour in love. On the one hand: 'when young and old receive this, they receive the light for their life; they understand why they live and they emerge from emptiness, noise and hedonistic enslavement; they leave mindless despair behind and

* Original Italian publication *Imparare a vivere*, art. in 'Città Nuova', no.1, 1980

establish themselves on the ground of true life'. But Foco also sees the wider effect of this on society: 'The traders in immorality will be ruined commercially, along with arms dealers, the spokesmen for narrow interests, the worshippers of spiritual acidity nourished by hatred'. And in a typical Foco comment, accompanied by that inimitable smile, he adds: 'unless of course they too open themselves to the joy of the whole life'.

This magnificent ideal of communion with God and with our brother has social consequences which Foco describes in terms drawn from the study of the Fathers of the Church. All goods belong to God. All men should live on these goods in work, in love, sharing in communion what is surplus. In that sharing we are not giving our own, we are giving 'what the poor is missing'.

A clear quotation from Justin's Apology (2nd century AD) clarifies the issue: 'We who previously used magic arts now consecrate ourselves to the good God. We who feasted wrongfully on the riches and fortunes of others now hold in common even the goods we possess and share them with all the poor. We who used to hate one another and kill one another and did not welcome people of other races and customs into our homes, now after the coming of Christ live together in community'.

Such a quote was self-evident and needed no commentary to make it relevant. It also describes rather well the life the Focolare live. But Foco was ready to push home the point that such teaching was not 'Communist' but 'truly Christian'. He believed that Marx and Engels had derived their teaching in some way from Christ, but that they had deformed the idea. The experience of Communism in Asia and Europe has not been progressive movement towards love and communion. It had led to conflict between peoples. 'If Christ is removed', he argues, 'the reason for living together is removed'. And he is quick to apply this to marriage.

The journalist honoured

In 1984, the Town Council of Tivoli instituted a prize entitled the *Igino Giordani Prize*. This will be awarded every year for outstanding contributions in the field of *'saggistica, letteratura e promozione umana'* (essays, literature and human development) in honour of Igino Giordani, born in Tivoli. The first person to receive the award was Chiara Lubich on 28th September 1984 in the Villa D'Este in Tivoli. The reason cited is because she 'more than any other person represents the ideal direction of Giordani'.

266

7

A New Dawn at Rocca di Papa

After Mya died, it was the most natural thing that Foco should move to Rocca di Papa and enter fully into the life of the Focolare to which he had belonged for years. While Mya lived, Foco was a married man, and in her final weakness he nursed her night and day with utter devotion and love. After she died and following a period of mourning, in agreement with his children, he came home to Rocca di Papa as a consecrated member of the Focolare. On 4th May 1974, he came with his few belongings to live the Ideal from within a community of dedicated men. As a married focolarino he had claimed the right to full membership. He was assigned to a focolare at Rocca di Papa together with Antonio Petrilli, Ezio Tancini and Mario Brini. All there were celibate members living in complete dedication to their vocation as members of the Movement.

Igino Giordani had served the Movement well and understood it in all its depth. But in a certain sense he had lived it from the outside, now he came in. He saw the life of the Focolare from the inside. It was a new experience for him. Igino asked for no special treatment. He wanted to live the life of a simple focolarino, like any other. The flat which belonged to his focolare was simply furnished and with the perfect taste that one finds throughout the

Movement. He lived having all things in common with other members and he worked. The study contained all he needed for the articles and books that he was still writing. There he received visitors and many came to seek his advice or to interview for a newspaper.

When I asked Antonio, who shared his life with Foco in the focolare at the Mariapolis Centre at Rocca di Papa, what the move had meant, he listed a number of things that became possible only after his move.

His presence at Rocca di Papa was a powerful contribution to the influence of that centre upon the Movement. He was available. The many conferences held there could avail themselves of his wisdom. Quietly he would descend to the great joy of the participants, sometimes just to listen, often to gather around him groups who would ply him with questions. The younger they were the better.

Foco and the young

Chiara had called the young members *gen*. They are the new generation of Focolare. Besides the gen 2 (the second generation of the Focolare Movement), going progressively younger, are the gen 3 and the gen 4. Just before his death, when he was already 85, he wrote a letter to his beloved gen 3, who at that time were members aged 7 to 13:

Dear gen 3,
Since, I'm a gen 3 too, I would like to share with you an experience of mine. Yesterday I was taking a walk in the garden with a Franciscan priest. He said to me that I kept young. And I told him that no one would believe me when I repeated what he said, unless I had it in writing. Jesus tells us we have to be like children. We have to be in the 'new man' every moment of the day in order to

remain always young. Our revolution rejects all that is 'old'. This has to be our rule: 'It is forbidden to become old'.

How can we always stay young? Simply by always loving.

Gandhi once started crying in front of the cross and said: 'He who does not have the love that Jesus had, becomes old, becomes like a dead person'. This is true because a life without Jesus is the life of a dead person. But gen 3 when I am with you, I always find joy, because we love God and we love one another. These two loves go together. Every neighbour helps us to get closer to God.

So, let us always remain young! I wish that you may always keep your youthfulness and never become old.

Foco

It was in that period that I knew him best and I can testify to his sense of eternal youth. Physically his body was weak. Long car journeys were a strain upon his resources. But both mentally and spiritually he retained the youthful striving and the excitement at new growth and new love. With the children under 7 – the gen 4 – he was very specially happy and he constantly recalled that 'of such is the kingdom of God'.

The editor of 'Città Nuova'

Igino Giordani was an experienced editor as well as a prolific writer, before he came to the Focolare Movement. It was obvious that when he did he would edit the journal of the Movement. This was called 'Città Nuova' and he was its first editor for twenty four years. His successor, Guglielmo Boselli, who worked closely with him in his closing years wrote of his over-riding principle:

As editor he affirmed the close interdependence which

exists between human advancement and the relationship with the divine in a short phrase, 'Father in heaven and bread on earth'.

The last six years of his editorship were at Rocca di Papa and he did not relax the hold of a strong editor. Many helped him as he grew older and it is a tribute to the magazine, which was published fortnightly that it never fell from the high standards he had maintained.

The fortnightly magazine is an extraordinary example of the breadth of interest he inspired in the Movement. It is not simply a journal of the activities of the Focolare Movement, it is a journal which enables the members to think responsibly about the issues of the day.

The publishing house

Apart from this fortnightly magazine, Città Nuova is also the publishing house of the Movement. It has an established reputation as a Christian publishing house and several similar presses have sprung up in other parts of the world. Città Nuova has published several of Giordani's books, often putting the earlier books into paperback and giving them an attractive appearance.

The end and the beginning of life

For the last six years of his life, Foco lived as a focolarino at Rocca di Papa. They were inevitably years of physical decline. At 76 he had already lived far longer than most people expected, but his indomitable spirit and his lively interest in almost everything kept him young. There is a youth about the Movement that was reflected in the ageing Igino Giordani.

Gradually he had to reduce his programme, but never his interest. He grew to anticipate death with excitement. The worn out body and the pain of ancient wounds were a burden at times. He became tired when he wanted to continue and his focolare protected him from undue strain.

Although I was allowed to see him and talk with him whenever I was there, a gentle hand restrained me from over-tiring him. It was easy to tell. Igino began in English and as he grew more tired he lapsed first into Italian and then used his eyes to communicate. They were eyes of hope. He longed for that closer fellowship with Mary and with Christ that only death could bring him. He was not impatient and he loved life with all its exciting facets. Yet as the years went by he was weary and longed for his proper home.

Shortly after Christmas 1979, Igino was unable to go further in his earthly pilgrimage. The Focolare prepared for his departure. I was in the midst of writing this book and had always had the greatest help from all the members of the Movement, especially from Enzo Fondi and Gabriella Fallacara. Without this attentive help this book would have been quite impossible. I was progressing well and had arranged to visit Rome in 1980 and read through some copies of 'Fides' in Rocca di Papa. Igino had put aside some papers for me to read and although I knew him to be ill, I had hoped to do a little work and see him.

The end was signalled to me by a sad letter from Gabriella Fallacara, which remains one of my treasures. It was on Centro Uno paper, dated 26.2.80:

Dear Mr. Robertson,

I received your letter in which you conveyed your participation in this trial that Foco is passing and we together with him. Thank you.

I understand from your letter that you want to come to Rome all the same. So as not to disappoint you when you arrive I want to let you know the exact state of things. Since Foco took ill we have not touched his papers at Centro Uno for any reason – according to Foco's instructions – so that when you come we cannot give you any.

Foco's flat at Centro Mariapolis is practically transformed into a clinic: none of the focolarini who assist Foco sleep, work or eat there. They only enter when it is their turn of assistance. This means that you cannot even go into the flat to read Foco's books etc. The Doctors, who predict a long recovery under their special attention, have ordered this.

In spite of my personal wish to see you both, I would advise you to postpone your visit to Rome, so that at another time you would be able to profit more. We are always willing to help you find a suitable pension at another time.

It has cost me a lot to write this letter to you, because I know it will slow up your writing of the book and delay other work, but on the other hand we are only now able to give an objective valuation of the situation.

However, we think that this difficulty will be something to offer to God – 'Per Te' – and this is the best present to give to Foco.

If you really want to come all the same, we could just let you read Foco's articles published in 'Città Nuova', 'Gen' and 'Gen's' that we have at Centro Uno.

I hope you received 'Città Nuova'. Foco made a subscription for you just before he took ill.

Gabri Fallacara

The whole scene was at once vividly portrayed, and although I was deeply moved by it, I went to Rome with my wife on 17th March and we stayed with the Swedish Sisters at Santa Brigida in Piazza Farnese. I did not see Igino during that short visit, but I wanted to be in Rome while he was dying. There was an extraordinary sense of peace as we explored Rome and were surrounded by the presence of our beloved Igino. In some way, I believe he knew that we were with him. After 8 days we left Rome and I knew that I should not see Igino again in this life. I put the papers to one side for a year to give me time to accept this loss.

On 18th April 1980. Igino died. The telegram from Gabriella Fallacara read quite simply:

> Foco died serenely,
> *Gabri*

God was his only love

When I talked with Antonio Petrilli, who had been close to him in the focolare and who always watched over him with great care, I told him of my bereavement. He understood, but said that he never missed 'Foco'. This was no callous forgetting of his friend, but as he assured me: 'He has never left this flat. His presence and his love for God unites us all still'. He confessed to being overwhelmed occasionally at the thought that Foco would not be seen or heard in the flat, but soon he insisted Foco comforted him and 'he is working harder for us now than ever'.

It was Antonio who gave me the liveliest picture of that new dawn at Rocca di Papa. 'It is not easy', he said, 'for those of us who lived close to him to describe all that his presence meant to us. For six years he insisted on calling himself a simple focolarino, yet we felt more like his disciples'.

Antonio recalled how he would sit on one of the seats in the garden of the Mariapolis Centre and crowds would gather round him to see him and ask questions just to hear him speak. He never tired of telling of his meeting with Chiara and the Movement, of what he called his 'deepest experiences of God'.

It was, of course, the last months of his life that I was most interested to hear about. Antonio said that they were a most tremendous lesson for all who were close to him. 'He left us the most eloquent pages of his story although unable to write'. This was the period when he gave living witness to the faith and to the ideals that had inspired his whole life. 'Those months were his living legacy'.

Anna Maria Zanzucchi, who together with her husband had worked with Igino in the New Families Movement and particularly in his preparation of engaged couples, went to visit him a few days before his death. 'We brought him', she writes, 'all the love and prayers of the married focolarini and the families in the Movement. Looking at us with his keen gaze, he said: "This is the most beautiful innovation in our whole Movement. It will be the salvation of society. Everything is of use, also your sacrifices. It is done now, for the most part. Now I can leave . . . " '

Igino had a great capacity for love and this was shown in many ways throughout his life in family and among friends. But his love for God was of a different kind – it was the source of all the other loves. He put this most clearly himself: 'All that is happening to me is actually God's love. It is happening because I have loved God, because I had no other love but him, nothing else'. This discounts neither his love for Mya, nor his love for his children. For them it was a derived love, springing from his enduring love for God. He had said, long ago that union meant not just being with God, but it meant unity, a unity with those he loved in God.

Antonio Petrilli

Four years after the death of Foco, I was sitting in his flat in Rocca di Papa. It was tidier than when he worked there. All the books were carefully numbered and arranged in the cupboard by the loving hands of Antonio. It was then that he told me that he did not miss Foco because he was always there. We looked out of the window on to the garden where a seat was empty. We remembered and for a moment I thought I saw Igino waiting for us to assemble around him. Antonio began to talk of the last months:

> Even when his illness kept him bedridden, he still wanted to particpate in our life together in the focolare. He always wanted to join us at mealtimes. When he did his presence compelled us to live in such a way that the reality of the focolare – Jesus in our midst – would never be missing. We had a wonderful experience of strengthening him – the more our mutual love and unity grew, the more he felt strengthened by Jesus in our midst. In fact he became a kind of thermometer of our unity. One day, he voiced what we all felt: 'Our coming together in this divine life is an extraordinary source of strength'. . . During the last period before his death, it seemed as though two poles of his life – his natural family and the focolare – had become one reality.

In these last days, his greatest happiness was to see the bonds of love strengthening between his children and the members of his focolare. His face, Antonio told me, beamed with happiness when the family came and they joined with the focolare around his bed:

> For him, love had made us all his children and all brothers in God: one family.

The closing weeks

As the illness progressed those who lived with him served him like priests at an altar. The many things that have to be done for a man in the last days of weakness were, as Antonio said, 'like an act of service and love to Christ crucified'. This reached its climax when they celebrated Mass in his room. 'It seemed as though the supernatural atmosphere reached its highest peak at that moment'. When he was asked at what time he wished to receive Jesus in the Eucharist, however weak and tired he was, he always replied: 'Right now!'

'How lucky I am', he told those serving him, 'being able to receive Communion here at home every day'.

His last 'sermon' came on 30th January 1980, quite short, but summing up his life's quest:

> Christ unites us to himself through the Eucharist which is Love, and through suffering which is divinized love. Thus the commandment of the Last Supper keeps being transmitted and lived. Christ redeemed us with suffering and continues to redeem us through suffering and love.

The Pope's blessing brought to him by Chiara was his last treasure. It was framed and hung where he could see it. Now, he felt as though this gift from the Pope was the Church's response to this love.

Another thought on his mind at the end was contained in a sentence which Antonio tells us he repeated again and again: 'He who sees his brother sees the Lord'. This 'charity', this love for Jesus in his neighbour was so much part of him that even towards the end, when he was in need of everything, he continued giving of himself to others. Those who were there to help him ended up being helped.

Antonio was deeply moved as he remembered those last days:

His love for Christ was so deeply rooted that those around him were unaware of his daily suffering as he offered up his illness to God. This love absorbed all suffering and transformed it into itself. Only on occasion, when he dictated some of his thoughts, we realized how his peace sprang from the depth of his suffering. One of these dictated thoughts was on 15th January:

We have never been so much one with Jesus as we are now when, crucified with him, we can give him the joy of our living participation.

The last salute

Surrounded by both his families and held in love and deepest esteem by multitudes, Igino Giordani died on 18th April 1980 in the Mariapolis Centre at Rocca di Papa.

Just before dying he regained consciousness for a few moments and gave a marvellous smile. Chiara commented: 'It seemed to us that this was a sign of that Paradise to which he was drawing near'. The coffin lay in the chapel there for three days and then a great crowd gathered around as the body of Igino was laid to rest.

His granddaughter, Simona, laid a bouquet of flowers on the coffin. His children, relatives, Chiara, leaders of the Focolare Movement, representatives of various Christian Churches, Members of Parliament, civil authorities, television reporters, journalists, and a great multitude of friends bore witness to his wide influence as they stood silently in the crowd.

Expressions of sorrow and condolence had already poured in. Two will suffice to represent the loss that Italy and the world sustained in his passing.

Vatican City, April 19th 1980

Upon hearing the sorrowful news of the death of Igino Giordani, beloved father and professor, the Holy Father recollected himself in fervent prayer for the repose of this chosen soul. He dearly recalls this illustrious figure who gave an unshakable witness of Christian faith in our time, through an exemplary and diligent life based on the Gospel and numerous apologetic writings on doctrine full of wisdom. As a sign of his benevolence, the Holy Father heartily imparts to all his children, relatives and friends the comforting apostolic blessing, as a sign of that hope which does not deceive.

Cardinal Casaroli, Secretary of State.

Rome, April 21st 1980

I was deeply saddened by the news of the death of Igino Giordani, with whom I felt a deep friendship. I am moved as I remember him today – a noble person with a high moral and democratic conscience. In this moment of sorrow I wish to express to his family and relatives my condolences and heartfelt sympathy.

Sandro Pertini, President of the Italian Republic.

278

Finale

28th September 1984: The Igino Giordani Prize

Only four days after what would have been his ninetieth
birthday, the memory of Igino Giordani was celebrated
at Tivoli with the first award of the Igino Giordani Prize,
given by unanimous consent to Chiara Lubich. In the
magnificent surroundings of the Villa D'Este, which he
knew so well, Chiara described the man. No one had
known him better and none had influenced him more.
And among the many people who thanked God for Igino
Giordani, few had more reason to be grateful than the
founder of the Movement to which he had given the half
of his lifetime and the whole of his devotion: the
Focolare. It was of Foco that she spoke and compared his
saintly character to the demands of the Sermon on the
Mount:

Someone once said that if the Gospel disappeared from
every part of the earth, the Christian should be such that
if anyone saw his or her life, it would be possible to
rewrite the Gospel.

Well then, Giordani was one of these Christians. When
he departed this life, the day that all gathered around him
for their final farewell – and there were thousands from
all over the world – that appropriate passage of the
Gospel was read: the Beatitudes. All who knew him well
agreed in affirming that he had lived them all.

He was indeed 'pure in heart' in an exceptional way. It

279

was this purity that made him describe man's earthly existence, since it is always watched over by God's providential love (in good fortune and in what is called misfortune) as a divine adventure.

It was this purity of heart that refined his most sacred feelings and gave them power to realize their potential. He had a tremendous love for his wife. And it was moving and impressive to see the intensity of his affection for his four children, as for his grandchildren, such that he showed himself to be a perfect father, a perfect grandfather, as well as a man totally of God.

He was 'poor in spirit' because of his complete detachment from all he possessed, but above all from all he was.

His heart was laden with 'mercy': in his presence, even the most miserable sinner felt himself forgiven and the most destitute felt himself a king.

He was a 'peacemaker', as documented by his career as a politician.

He reached such a possession of 'meekness' as to make one understand why the Gospel says that who possesses this virtue will inherit the earth: with his great gentleness, his courteous way of treating people, expressing himself as only he knew how, he soon captivated all those he came across, because they felt at ease with him, considered with dignity. Young people related to him as equals, and not infrequently one heard people say, particularly in his later years, that from this person radiated something of the supernatural.

He experienced the beatitude of affliction, both spiritually and physically ('Blessed are they who mourn', said Jesus), because, as he was well rooted in the mystery of the cross, he knew how to transform by a divine alchemy – as he said – suffering into love.

Like all true Christians, he truly 'hungered and thirsted for righteousness' sake' and struggled for it all his life.

He also suffered 'persecution' in God's name, so that we today believe him to be in possession of his kingdom.

Yes, you could read the Gospel in him. The Gospel, also, of becoming 'like little children'.

A Christian of the first order, a scholar, an apologist,

an apostle. When it seemed to him that he came upon a spring of living water, gushing up from the Church, a new testimony that the Holy Spirit is always alive and active in her, he knew how to put everything aside in order to follow Jesus who called him to quench his thirst with that water.

He also lived the Gospel of humility. When he thought that someone in our Movement, having regard for his past accomplishments, wanted to reserve special privilges for him, he begged to be treated like all the others.

But in Giordani what was characteristic was especially the Gospel of love.

Athirst for God from his childhood, yet called to live in the midst of the world, he discovered a way to reach the Eternal, a way that is sure as perhaps no other is. It was, as he describes it, in three stages, almost three points of a triangle: myself, my brother, God. He was convinced that he would reach God by loving his brother, by means of his brother, serving all those brothers he met in the course of the day.

This is what he did and he reached great heights. Because the more he loved his brothers, the more in his spirit he found union with God. And vice versa, the more he was united with God, the more refined was his charity towards his neighbour.

For this reason he was great as a Christian. He had hit squarely upon that Gospel law which is a kind of little summary of all the others: love for one's neighbour.

But if Giordani was a true Christian, he was also a special Christian. God called him, in fact, to be a co-founder of a new work in the Church to which he made an irreplaceable contribution in the last thirty-two years of his life.

He had always looked for a way to open in the direction of the desire, that consumed his soul, to be totally consecrated to God, even though he was in the married state. He had sought hard and then, in 1948, he came across the Focolare Movement, just five years after its birth.

It was he who opened up the focolares (the centres that animated the Movement which until then were formed of celibates only) to married people, who followed him in hungering for sanctity and consecration. Thus was brought into effect the project which previously had only been vaguely foreseen: virgins and married people living together – insofar as their states in life allowed – based upon the model of the family of Nazareth.

It was he who gave an impulse to the birth of the Movement's 'mass movements' such as the New Families, in which the couple make a tiny living church from the cell of their family, and New Humanity which strives to animate with a genuine Christian spirit the worlds of work, art, medicine, education, politics and so forth.

It was he who was the personification of one of the most important aims of this Movement: to contribute to the reunification of the Churches.

It was he who above all helped the Movement to put down strong roots into the Church, so that he saw it, even in his lifetime, spread its branches in five continents and come to be present in more than 140 nations, with all the good one can imagine if one considers its evangelical spirit which underlines universal brotherhood, respect and mutual love, unity among all men, things that are so needed in these times tormented by tensions, discriminations, divisions, wars.

Giordani was one of the greatest gifts heaven has given to the Focolare Movement.

He lavished the greater part of his life upon this new reality in the Church, which also has another name: the Work of Mary. 'Of Mary' because it seems to us that here, as at other times and in other places on earth, it is above all Mary, the Virgin, the Mother of the Church and of humanity, who is at work.

And it appears to us that Mary, with whom he was in love, rewarded him by making him a chosen one of hers, indeed transporting him almost into the sphere of the mystics.

St. Louis Grignion de Montfort, speaking of these people whom the Virgin loves in a special way, says that the principal gift they acquire is the realization, here below, of her life in their souls, in such a way that it is no longer the soul that lives, but Mary lives in it or, if you like, the soul of Mary becomes theirs.

Chiara continued by quoting from Igino Giordani's 'Diary of Fire', the account of the mystical experience, to which we already refered at length in an earlier chapter. It is the entry for 6th October 1957. He concludes that account with 'her presence had . . . virginized my soul'. Chiara comments:

And we think we see something of the sanctity of Igino Giordani among these gathered fragments of his life. This is Igino Giordani: a true follower of Christ, a man of God.

Also by

Edwin Robertson

CHIARA

Edwin Robertson's biography of the foundress of the Focolare Movement is a fascinating story of how one person from humble origins can, quietly and unassumingly, have a tremendous impact upon the world. By simply trying to be faithful to God who had captured her heart, Chiara began her life's adventure during the destruction of the Second World War and found that she was an instrument by which a new voice was heard. This voice proclaimed something craved by all: unity. For at all levels there is the need for unity: to draw friends together and cure the sadness of being unloved and forgotten; to reunite families threatened by divorce and separation; to create harmony in society so as to overcome racism and discrimination against the disadvantaged; and to bring the nations into an effective community of shared policy and concern so that they can tackle the problems of pollution, disputed sovereignty, the unjust distribution of wealth, and the agony of war. Chiara's ideal, centred in the experience of being united in the name of Jesus, gives a powerful contribution to the achievement of unity at all these levels.

The book tells the story of this remarkable person in simple terms. Her life is a clear witness to a limpid and deep spirituality.

Through his description, Edwin Robertson also fills out details helpful in understanding the background to the life of Igino Giordani.

Available from:

New City
57 Twyford Avenue
London W3 9PZ

Igino Giordani

DIARY OF FIRE

Igino Giordani's deeply spiritual reflections on his own life
speak to everyone. As he came to terms, in the pages of his
diary, with his own passions and egoism, Giordani in effect
unmasked the unworthy motives that govern the lives of each
of us – and he overcame them.

His diary, as a consequence, became a series of meditations
that, step by step, scale the heights of holiness. But the path
they take is one that all can follow and all can learn from. For
Giordani was a man for everyone, a lay person and the father of
a family, highly gifted certainly, but one who struggled with
the universal difficulties every human being must face.

This is the book in which Giordani reveals his heart. It takes
us on a journey that ends in one place: God.

About Giordani, Dr Klaus Hemmerle, Roman Catholic
Bishop of Aachen said:

> *If someone were to ask me what is virginity, I think I would
> have to speak about Giordani, a married man. I would have to
> speak about how he understood and loved virginity, the giving
> of oneself to God alone, life in God alone. From this he drew the
> courage of his decision and strength: holiness is the vocation and
> path which is open to all in Christ.*
>
> *If someone were to ask me to show him heaven, I believe that
> I would answer 'I have seen Paradise in Giordani's eyes and in
> his heart.' Yes, in the eyes and heart of a politician. He lived in
> heaven and so his hands were free for the earth.*

Available from:

New City
57 Twyford Avenue
London W3 9PZ